LINUX ADMIN

For Absolute Beginners

Martin Stevenson

INTRODUCTION

Linux was designed based on the Unix philosophy of "small, precise tools chained together simplifying larger tasks". Linux, at its root, does not have large single-purpose applications for one specific use a lot of the time. Instead, there are hundreds of basic utilities that when combined offer great power to accomplish big tasks with efficiency. Unique amongst business class Linux distributions, CentOS stays true to the open-source nature that Linux was founded on. This book gives a complete understanding on Linux Admin and explains how to use it for benefit.

AUDIENCE

This book has been prepared for beginners to help them understand the fundamentals of Linux Admin. It will specifically be useful for Linux administration professionals. After completing this tutorial, you will find yourself at a moderate level of expertise from where you can take yourself to the next levels.

PREREQUISITES

Before you go ahead, we assume that you have a basic knowledge of Linux and Administration fundamentals.

TABLE OF CONTENTS

Introduction..iii

Audience iv

Prerequisites..v

Linux Admin - CentOS Overview 1

Basic CentOS Linux Commands..2

    Examples of the Linux Philosophy 2

Linux Admin - File / Folder Management..4

    Applying Permissions to Directories and Files 4

        chmod : Change File Mode Permission Bits 6

        chown : Change File Owner and Group..6

        chgrp : Change Group Ownership of File or Directory 6

        Real-world practice..6

        umask Command: Supplies the Default Modes for File and Directory

        Permissions As They are Created..7

Linux Admin - User Management 9

    CentOS Users 9

        Disabling User Accounts..10

    Manage Groups..10

Linux Admin - Quota Management 13

    Enable Quota Management in /etc/fstab..13

        Reconfiguring Kernel Boot Options for XFS File Systems 14

    Remount the File System..15

    Create Quota Database Files...15

    Add Quota Limits Per User 16

Systemd Services Start and Stop...18

    Manage Services with systemctl..19

        Basic systemctl Usage 19

        Stopping a Service 20

Linux Admin - Resource Mgmt with systemctl 22

    status 22

    list-units 23

    is-active 24

    cat 24

Linux Admin - Resource Mgmt with crgoups 25

    Polite CPU Service 1...25

    Evil CPU Service 2..26

    Configure CGroups in CentOS Linux..27

Linux Admin - Process Management 28

    Work with Processes 28
  Basic CentOS Process and Job Management in CentOS 28
    nohup 29
    ps Command 29
    pstree Command 30
    top Command 31
    kill Command 32
    free Command 33
    nice Command 34
    renice 34
  Linux Admin - Firewall Setup 35

Configure PHP in CentOS Linux 40

  Install MySQL Database Server 41
    mariadb-server.x86_64 41
    mariadb-devel.x86_64 41
    mariadb.x86_64 41
    mariadb-libs.x86_64 41
  Install and Configure PHP 42
Set Up Python with CentOS Linux 44

Configure Ruby on CentOS Linux 47

  Method 1 : rbenv for Dynamic Ruby Development Environments 47
  Method 2 : Install Ruby from CentOS Packages 48
  Linux Admin - Set Up Perl for CentOS Linux 49

Install and Configure Open LDAP 52

  Brief History of LDAP 52
  Install Open LDAP on CentOS 53
  Configure Open LDAP 54
  Configure LDAP Client Access 58
Linux Admin - Create SSL Certificates 59

    TLS and SSL Background 59
  SSL vs TLS Versioning 59
  Install and Configure openssl 60
  Create Self-signed Certificate for OpenLDAP 61
  Create Self-signed Certificate for Apache Web Server 61
  Configure Apache to Use Key and Certificate Files 63
    SSLProtocol 64
    Specify path to our self-signed certificate file 64
Install Apache Web Server CentOS 7 65

  Brief History on Apache WebServer 65
  Install Current Stable Version on CentOS Linux 7 65
    Listening host and port 66

Listen 66
DocumentRoot 66
Linux Admin - MySQL Setup On CentOS 7 68

MariaDB vs MySQL On CentOS Linux 68
Download and Add the MySQL Repository 68
Set Up Postfix MTA and IMAP/POP3 70

Install the "cyrus-sasl* package 72
Configure /etc/postfix/main.cf for SASL Auth 72
My SASL Options in main.conf 72
Install Dovecot IMAP and POP3 Server 72
Enable protocols and daemon service for dovecot 73
Linux Admin - Install Anonymous FTP 75

Create a root FTP directory 76
Change owner and group of FTP root to ftp 76
Configure /etc/vsftpd/vsftpd.conf" 76
Linux Admin - Remote Management 78

Remote Console Management 78
Remote GUI Management 78
Laying the Foundation for Security with SSH for Remote Console Access 78
Install and Configure SSH for Remote Access 79
Configure VNC for Remote CentOS Administration 81
Set Up SSH Tunnel Through VNC 83
Use SSH Tunnel for Remote X-Windows 84
Linux Admin - Traffic Monitoring in CentOS 86

Traffic Monitoring for LAN / WAN Scenarios 86
Install Fedora EPEL Repository — Extra Packages for Enterprise Linux 86
Install and Use nload 88
Linux Admin - Log Management 91

Set the Correct System Time Zone 91
Use journalctl to Analyze Logs 92
Examine Boot Logs 92
Configure Boot Location for Persistent Boot Logs 93
Analyze Logs by Log Type 94
Linux Admin - Backup and Recovery 96

3-2-1 Backup Strategy 96
System Recovery 96
Use rsync for File Level Backups 97
When to use rsync 98
Local Backup With rsync 98
Remote Differential Backups With rsync 99
Use DD for Block-by-Block Bare Metal Recovery Images 100
Use gzip and tar for Secure Storage 103
Using Gnu Tar in CentOS Linux 103
Use gzip to Compress File Backups 105

Encrypt TarBall Archives 107
    Install 7zip on Centos 107
Linux Admin - System Updates 109

    Manually Update CentOS 7..109
    Configure Automatic Updates for YUM 112
Linux Admin - Shell Scripting..114

    Introduction to Bash Shell...114
    Using Shell Script Versus Scripting Language...114
    Shell 115
    Scripting Language 115
    Input Output and Redirection 116
    STDOUT...117
    STDIN 117
    The pipe character " | "..118
    Redirecting Output with & 118
    Bash Shell Constructs...118
    BASH Troubleshooting Hints 119
Linux Admin - Package Management 120

    YUM Package Manager 120
    yum check-update 120
    yum update 121
    Install Software via YUM..121
    Most Common YUM Commands 121
    Install Software with YUM..121
    Graphical Package Management in CentOS...125
Linux Admin - Volume Management 126

    Traditional Linux Disk Administration Tools..126
    Create a Disk Label..127
    Create the Partitions on the Disk 127
    Make the File System 128
    Create Volume Groups and Logical Volumes 129

LINUX ADMIN - CENTOS OVERVIEW

Unique among business class Linux distributions, CentOS stays true to the open-source nature that Linux was founded on. The first Linux kernel was developed by a college student at the University of Helsinki (Linus Torvalds) and combined with the GNU utilities founded and promoted by Richard Stallman. CentOS has a proven, open-source licensing that can power today's business world.

CentOS has quickly become one of the most prolific server platforms in the world. Any Linux Administrator, when seeking employment, is bound to come across the words: "CentOS Linux Experience Preferred". From startups to Fortune 10 tech titans, CentOS has placed itself amongst the higher echelons of server operating systems worldwide.

What makes CentOS stand out from other Linux distributions is a great combination of −

- ❖ Open source licensing
- ❖ Dedicated user-base of Linux professionals
- ❖ Good hardware support
- ❖ Rock-solid stability and reliability
- ❖ Focus on security and updates
- ❖ Strict adherence to software packaging standards needed in a corporate environment

Before starting the lessons, we assume that the readers have a basic knowledge of Linux and Administration fundamentals such as −

- ❖ What is the root user?
- ❖ The power of the root user
- ❖ Basic concept of security groups and users
- ❖ Experience using a Linux terminal emulator
- ❖ Fundamental networking concepts
- ❖ Fundamental understanding of interpreted programming languages (Perl, Python, Ruby)
- ❖ Networking protocols such as HTTP, LDAP, FTP, IMAP, SMTP
- ❖ Cores that compose a computer operating system: file system, drivers, and the kerne

BASIC CENTOS LINUX COMMANDS

Before learning the tools of a CentOS Linux Administrator, it is important to note the philosophy behind the Linux administration command line.

Linux was designed based on the Unix philosophy of "small, precise tools chained together simplifying larger tasks". Linux, at its root, does not have large single-purpose applications for one specific use a lot of the time. Instead, there are hundreds of basic utilities that when combined offer great power to accomplish big tasks with efficiency.

Examples of the Linux Philosophy

For example, if an administrator wants a listing of all the current users on a system, the following chained commands can be used to get a list of all system users. On execution of the command, the users are on the system are listed in an alphabetical order.

```
[root@centosLocal centos]# cut /etc/passwd -d":" -f1 | sort
abrt
adm
avahi
bin
centos
chrony
colord
daemon
dbus
```

It is easy to export this list into a text file using the following command.

```
[root@localhost /]# cut /etc/passwd -d ":" -f1 > system_users.txt
[root@localhost /]# cat ./system_users.txt | sort | wc –l
40
[root@localhost /]#
```

It is also possible to compare the user list with an export at a later date.

```
[root@centosLocal centos]# cut /etc/passwd -d ":" -f1 > system_users002.txt &&
   cat system_users002.txt | sort | wc -l
41
[root@centosLocal centos]# diff ./system_users.txt ./system_users002.txt
evilBackdoor [root@centosLocal centos]#
```

With this approach of small tools chained to accomplish bigger tasks, it is simpler to make a script performing these commands, than automatically email results at regular time intervals.

Basic Commands every Linux Administrator should be proficient in are –

- ❖ vim
- ❖ grep
- ❖ more and less
- ❖ tail
- ❖ head

- ❖ wc
- ❖ sort
- ❖ uniq
- ❖ tee
- ❖ cat
- ❖ cut
- ❖ sed
- ❖ tr
- ❖ paste

In the Linux world, Administrators use filtering commands every day to parse logs, filter command output, and perform actions with interactive shell scripts. As mentioned, the power of these commands come in their ability to modify one another through a process called piping.

The following command shows how many words begin with the letter a from the CentOS main user dictionary.

```
[root@centosLocal ~]# egrep '^a.*$' /usr/share/dict/words | wc -l
25192
[root@centosLocal ~]#
```

LINUX ADMIN - FILE / FOLDER MANAGEMENT

To introduce permissions as they apply to both directories and files in CentOS Linux, let's look at the following command output.

```
[centos@centosLocal etc]$ ls -ld /etc/yum*
drwxr-xr-x. 6 root root 100 Dec  5 06:59 /etc/yum
-rw-r--r--. 1 root root 970 Nov 15 08:30 /etc/yum.conf
drwxr-xr-x. 2 root root 187 Nov 15 08:30 /etc/yum.repos.d
```

Note — The three primary object types you will see are

- ❖ "-" — a dash for plain file
- ❖ "d" — for a directory
- ❖ "l" — for a symbolic link

We will focus on the three blocks of output for each directory and file —

- ❖ drwxr-xr-x : root : root
- ❖ -rw-r--r-- : root : root
- ❖ drwxr-xr-x : root : root

Now let's break this down, to better understand these lines —

d	Means the object type is a directory
rwx	Indicates directory permissions applied to the owner
r-x	Indicates directory permissions applied to the group
r-x	Indicates directory permissions applied to the world
root	The first instance, indicates the owner of the directory
root	The second instance, indicates the group to which group permissions are applied

Understanding the difference between owner, group and world is important. Not understanding this can have big consequences on servers that host services to the Internet.

Before we give a real-world example, let's first understand the permissions as they apply to directories and files.

Please take a look at the following table, then continue with the instruction.

Octal	Symbolic	Perm.	Directory
1	x	Execute	Enter the directory and access files
2	w	Write	Delete or modify the files in a directory
4	r	Read	List the files within the directory

Note — When files should be accessible for reading in a directory, it is common to apply read and execute permissions. Otherwise, the users will have difficulty working with the files. Leaving write disabled will assure files cannot be: renamed, deleted, copied over, or have permissions modified.

Applying Permissions to Directories and Files

When applying permissions, there are two concepts to understand —

- ❖ Symbolic Permissions
- ❖ Octal Permissions

In essence, each are the same but a different way to referring to, and assigning file permissions. For a quick guide, please study and refer to the following table –

	Read	Write	Execute
Octal	4	2	1
Symbolic	r	w	x

When assigning permissions using the octal method, use a 3 byte number such as: 760. The number 760 translates into: Owner: rwx; Group: rw; Other (or world) no permissions.

Another scenario: 733 would translate to: Owner: rwx; Group: wx; Other: wx.

There is one drawback to permissions using the Octal method. Existing permission sets cannot be modified. It is only possible to reassign the entire permission set of an object.

Now you might wonder, what is wrong with always re-assigning permissions? Imagine a large directory structure, for example /var/www/ on a production web-server. We want to recursively take away the w or write bit on all directories for Other. Thus, forcing it to be pro-actively added only when needed for security measures. If we re-assign the entire permission set, we take away all other custom permissions assigned to every sub-directory.

Hence, it will cause a problem for both the administrator and the user of the system. At some point, a person (or persons) would need to re-assign all the custom permissions that were wiped out by re-assigning the entire permission-set for every directory and object.

In this case, we would want to use the Symbolic method to modify permissions –

```
chmod -R o-w /var/www/
```

The above command would not "overwrite permissions" but modify the current permission sets. So get accustomed to using the best practice

- ❖ Octal only to assign permissions
- ❖ Symbolic to modify permission sets

It is important that a CentOS Administrator be proficient with both Octal and Symbolic permissions as permissions are important for the integrity of data and the entire operating system. If permissions are incorrect, the end result will be both sensitive data and the entire operating system will be compromised.

With that covered, let's look at a few commands for modifying permissions and object owner/members –

- ❖ chmod
- ❖ chown
- ❖ chgrp

❖ umask

chmod : Change File Mode Permission Bits

Command	Action
-c	Like verbose, but will only report the changes made
-v	Verbose, outputsthe diagnostics for every request made
-R	Recursively applies the operation on files and directories

chmod will allow us to change permissions of directories and files using octal or symbolic permission sets. We will use this to modify our assignment and uploads directories.

chown : Change File Owner and Group

Command	Action
-c	Like verbose, but will only report the changes made
-v	Verbose, outputsthe diagnostics for every request made
-R	Recursively applies the operation on files and directories

chown can modify both owning the user and group of objects. However, unless needing to modify both at the same time, using chgrp is usually used for groups.

chgrp : Change Group Ownership of File or Directory

Command	Action
-c	Like verbose, but will only report the changes
-v	Verbose, outputs the diagnostics for every request made
-R	Recursively, applies the operations on file and directories

chgrp will change the group owner to that supplied.

Real-world practice

Let's change all the subdirectory assignments in /var/www/students/ so the owning group is the students group. Then assign the root of students to the professors group. Later, make Dr. Terry Thomas the owner of the students directory, since he is tasked as being in-charge of all Computer Science academia at the school.

As we can see, when created, the directory is left pretty raw.

```
[root@centosLocal ~]# ls -ld /var/www/students/
drwxr-xr-x. 4 root root 40 Jan  9 22:03 /var/www/students/
[root@centosLocal ~]# ls -l /var/www/students/
total 0
drwxr-xr-x. 2 root root 6 Jan  9 22:03 assignments
drwxr-xr-x. 2 root root 6 Jan  9 22:03 uploads
[root@centosLocal ~]#
```

As Administrators we never want to give our root credentials out to anyone. But at the same time, we need to allow users the ability to do their job. So let's allow

Dr. Terry Thomas to take more control of the file structure and limit what students can do.

```
[root@centosLocal ~]# chown -R drterryt:professors /var/www/students/
[root@centosLocal ~]# ls -ld /var/www/students/
drwxr-xr-x. 4 drterryt professors 40 Jan  9 22:03 /var/www/students/
[root@centosLocal ~]# ls -ls /var/www/students/
total 0
0 drwxr-xr-x. 2 drterryt professors 6 Jan  9 22:03 assignments
0 drwxr-xr-x. 2 drterryt professors 6 Jan  9 22:03 uploads
[root@centosLocal ~]#
```

Now, each directory and subdirectory has an owner of drterryt and the owning group is professors. Since the assignments directory is for students to turn assigned work in, let's take away the ability to list and modify files from the students group.

```
[root@centosLocal ~]# chgrp students /var/www/students/assignments/ && chmod
736 /var/www/students/assignments/
[root@centosLocal assignments]# ls -ld /var/www/students/assignments/
drwx-wxrw-. 2 drterryt students 44 Jan  9 23:14 /var/www/students/assignments/
[root@centosLocal assignments]#
```

Students can copy assignments to the assignments directory. But they cannot list contents of the directory, copy over current files, or modify files in the assignments directory. Thus, it just allows the students to submit completed assignments. The CentOS filesystem will provide a date-stamp of when assignments turned in.

As the assignments directory owner –

```
[drterryt@centosLocal assignments]$ whoami
drterryt
[drterryt@centosLocal assignments]$ ls -ld /var/www/students/assignment
drwx-wxrw-. 2 drterryt students 44 Jan  9 23:14 /var/www/students/assignments/
[drterryt@centosLocal assignments]$ ls -l /var/www/students/assignments/
total 4
-rw-r--r--. 1 adama  students  0 Jan  9 23:14 myassign.txt
-rw-r--r--. 1 tammyr students 16 Jan  9 23:18 terryt.txt
[drterryt@centosLocal assignments]$
```

We can see, the directory owner can list files as well as modify and remove files.

umask Command: Supplies the Default Modes for File and Directory Permissions As They are Created

umask is an important command that supplies the default modes for File and Directory Permissions as they are created.

umask permissions use unary, negated logic.

Permission	Operation
0	Read, write, execute
1	Read and write
2	Read and execute
3	Read only
4	Read and execute

5	Write only
6	Execute only
7	No permissions

```
[adama@centosLocal umask_tests]$ ls -l ./
-rw-r--r--. 1 adama students 0 Jan 10 00:27 myDir
-rw-r--r--. 1 adama students 0 Jan 10 00:27 myFile.txt
[adama@centosLocal umask_tests]$ whoami
adama
[adama@centosLocal umask_tests]$ umask
0022
[adama@centosLocal umask_tests]$
```

Now, let's change the umask for our current user, and make a new file and directory.

```
[adama@centosLocal umask_tests]$ umask 077
[adama@centosLocal umask_tests]$ touch mynewfile.txt
[adama@centosLocal umask_tests]$ mkdir myNewDir
[adama@centosLocal umask_tests]$ ls -l
total 0
-rw-r--r--. 1 adama students 0 Jan 10 00:27 myDir
-rw-r--r--. 1 adama students 0 Jan 10 00:27 myFile.txt
drwx------. 2 adama students 6 Jan 10 00:35 myNewDir
-rw-------. 1 adama students 0 Jan 10 00:35 mynewfile.txt
```

As we can see, newly created files are a little more restrictive than before.

umask for users must should be changed in either −

❖ /etc/profile
❖ ~/bashrc

```
[root@centosLocal centos]# su adama
[adama@centosLocal centos]$ umask
0022
[adama@centosLocal centos]$
```

Generally, the default umask in CentOS will be okay. When we run into trouble with a default of 0022, is usually when different departments belonging to different groups need to collaborate on projects.

This is where the role of a system administrator comes in, to balance the operations and design of the CentOS operating system.

LINUX ADMIN - USER MANAGEMENT

When discussing user management, we have three important terms to understand-

- ❖ Users
- ❖ Groups
- ❖ Permissions

We have already discussed in-depth permissions as applied to files and folders. In this chapter, let's discuss about users and groups.

CentOS Users

In CentOS, there are two types accounts −

- ❖ System accounts − Used for a daemon or other piece of software.
- ❖ Interactive accounts − Usually assigned to a user for accessing system resources.

The main difference between the two user types is −

- ❖ System accounts are used by daemons to access files and directories. These will usually be disallowed from interactive login via shell or physical console login.
- ❖ Interactive accounts are used by end-users to access computing resources from either a shell or physical console login.

With this basic understanding of users, let's now create a new user for Bob Jones in the Accounting Department. A new user is added with the adduser command.

Following are some adduser common switches −

Switch	Action
-c	Adds comment to the user account
-m	Creates user home directory in default location, if nonexistent
-g	Default group to assign the user
-n	Does not create a private group for the user, usually a group with username
-M	Does not create a home directory
-s	Default shell other than /bin/bash
-u	Specifies UID (otherwise assigned by the system)
-G	Additional groups to assign the user to

When creating a new user, use the -c, -m, -g, -n switches as follows −

```
[root@localhost Downloads]# useradd -c "Bob Jones  Accounting Dept Manager"
-m -g accounting -n bjones
```

Now let's see if our new user has been created −

```
[root@localhost Downloads]# id bjones
(bjones) gid = 1001(accounting) groups = 1001(accounting)
[root@localhost Downloads]# grep bjones /etc/passwd
bjones:x:1001:1001:Bob Jones  Accounting Dept Manager:/home/bjones:/bin/bash
```

Now we need to enable the new account using the passwd command –

```
[root@localhost Downloads]# passwd bjones
Changing password for user bjones.
New password:
Retype new password:
passwd: all authentication tokens updated successfully.
[root@localhost Downloads]#
```

The user account is not enabled allowing the user to log into the system.

Disabling User Accounts

There are several methods to disable accounts on a system. These range from editing the /etc/passwd file by hand. Or even using the passwd command with the -lswitch. Both of these methods have one big drawback: if the user has ssh access and uses an RSA key for authentication, they can still login using this method.

Now let's use the chage command, changing the password expiry date to a previous date. Also, it may be good to make a note on the account as to why we disabled it.

```
[root@localhost Downloads]# chage -E 2005-10-01 bjones

[root@localhost Downloads]# usermod  -c "Disabled Account while Bob out of the country
for five months" bjones
[root@localhost Downloads]# grep bjones /etc/passwd
bjones:x:1001:1001:Disabled Account while Bob out of the country for four
months:/home/bjones:/bin/bash
[root@localhost Downloads]#
```

Manage Groups

Managing groups in Linux makes it convenient for an administrator to combine the users within containers applying permission-sets applicable to all group members. For example, all users in Accounting may need access to the same files. Thus, we make an accounting group, adding Accounting users.

For the most part, anything requiring special permissions should be done in a group. This approach will usually save time over applying special permissions to just one user. Example, Sally is in-charge of reports and only Sally needs access to certain files for reporting. However, what if Sally is sick one day and Bob does reports? Or the need for reporting grows? When a group is made, an Administrator only needs to do it once. The add users is applied as needs change or expand.

Following are some common commands used for managing groups –

- ❖ chgrp
- ❖ groupadd
- ❖ groups
- ❖ usermod

chgrp – Changes the group ownership for a file or directory.

Let's make a directory for people in the accounting group to store files and create directories for files.

```
[root@localhost Downloads]# mkdir /home/accounting
[root@localhost Downloads]# ls -ld /home/accounting
drwxr-xr-x. 2 root root 6 Jan 13 10:18 /home/accounting
[root@localhost Downloads]#
```

Next, let's give group ownership to the accounting group.

```
[root@localhost Downloads]# chgrp -v accounting /home/accounting/
changed group of '/home/accounting/' from root to accounting
[root@localhost Downloads]# ls -ld /home/accounting/
drwxr-xr-x. 2 root accounting 6 Jan 13 10:18 /home/accounting/
[root@localhost Downloads]#
```

Now, everyone in the accounting group has read and execute permissions to /home/accounting. They will need write permissions as well.

```
[root@localhost Downloads]# chmod g+w /home/accounting/
[root@localhost Downloads]# ls -ld /home/accounting/
drwxrwxr-x. 2 root accounting 6 Jan 13 10:18 /home/accounting/
[root@localhost Downloads]#
```

Since the accounting group may deal with sensitive documents, we need to apply some restrictive permissions for other or world.

```
[root@localhost Downloads]# chmod o-rx /home/accounting/
[root@localhost Downloads]# ls -ld /home/accounting/
drwxrwx---. 2 root accounting 6 Jan 13 10:18 /home/accounting/
[root@localhost Downloads]#
```

groupadd – Used to make a new group.

Switch	Action
-g	Specifies a GID for the group
-K	Overrides specs for GID in /etc/login.defs
-o	Allows overriding non-unique group id disallowance
-p	Group password, allowing the users to activate themselves

Let's make a new group called secret. We will add a password to the group, allowing the users to add themselves with a known password.

```
[root@localhost]# groupadd secret
[root@localhost]# gpasswd secret
Changing the password for group secret
New Password:
Re-enter new password:
[root@localhost]# exit
exit
[centos@localhost ~]$ newgrp secret
Password:
[centos@localhost ~]$ groups
secret wheel rdc
[centos@localhost ~]$
```

In practice, passwords for groups are not used often. Secondary groups are adequate and sharing passwords amongst other users is not a great security practice.

The groups command is used to show which group a user belongs to. We will use this, after making some changes to our current user.

usermod is used to update account attributes.

Following are the common usermod switches.

Switch	Action
-a	Appends, adds user to supplementary groups, only with the -G option
-c	Comment, updatesthe user comment value
-d	Home directory, updates the user's home directory
-G	Groups, adds or removesthe secondary user groups
-g	Group, default primary group of the user

```
[root@localhost]# groups centos
centos : accounting secret
[root@localhost]#
[root@localhost]# usermod -a -G wheel centos
[root@localhost]# groups centos
centos : accounting wheel secret
[root@localhost]#
```

LINUX ADMIN - QUOTA MANAGEMENT

CentOS disk quotas can be enabled both; alerting the system administrator and denying further disk-storage-access to a user before disk capacity is exceeded. When a disk is full, depending on what resides on the disk, an entire system can come to a screeching halt until recovered.

Enabling Quota Management in CentOS Linux is basically a 4 step process −

- ❖ Step 1 − Enable quota management for groups and users in /etc/fstab.
- ❖ Step 2 − Remount the filesystem.
- ❖ Step 3 − Create Quota database and generate disk usage table.
- ❖ Step 4 − Assign quota policies.

Enable Quota Management in /etc/fstab

First, we want to backup our /etc/fstab filen −

```
[root@centosLocal centos]# cp -r /etc/fstab ./
```

We now have a copy of our known working /etc/fstab in the current working directory.

```
#
# /etc/fstab
# Created by anaconda on Sat Dec 17 02:44:51 2016
#
# Accessible filesystems, by reference, are maintained under '/dev/disk'
# See man pages fstab(5), findfs(8), mount(8) and/or blkid(8) for more info
#
/dev/mapper/cl-root      /      xfs    defaults            0 0
UUID = 4b9a40bc-9480-4   /boot  xfs    defaults              0 0
/dev/mapper/cl-home      /home  xfs    defaults,usrquota,grpquota  0 0
/dev/mapper/cl-swap      swap   swap   defaults            0 0
```

We made the following changes in the options section of /etc/fstab for the volume or Label to where quotas are to be applied for users and groups.

- ❖ usrquota
- ❖ grpquota

As you can see, we are using the xfs filesystem. When using xfs there are extra manual steps involved. /home is on the same disk as /. Further investigation shows / is set for noquota, which is a kernel level mounting option. We must re-configure our kernel boot options.

```
root@localhost rdc]# mount | grep ' / '
/dev/mapper/cl-root on / type xfs (rw,relatime,seclabel,attr2,inode64,noquota)
[root@localhost rdc]#
```

Reconfiguring Kernel Boot Options for XFS File Systems

This step is only necessary under two conditions –

- ❖ When the disk/partition we are enabling quotas on, is using the xfs file system
- ❖ When the kernel is passing no quota parameter to /etc/fstab at boot time

Step 1 – Make a backup of /etc/default/grub.

```
cp /etc/default/grub ~/
```

Step 2 – Modify /etc/default/grub.

Here is the default file.

```
GRUB_TIMEOUT=5
GRUB_DISTRIBUTOR="$(sed 's, release .*$,,g' /etc/system-release)"
GRUB_DEFAULT=saved
GRUB_DISABLE_SUBMENU=true
GRUB_TERMINAL_OUTPUT="console"
GRUB_CMDLINE_LINUX="crashkernel=auto rd.lvm.lv=cl/root rd.lvm.lv=cl/swap rhgb quiet"
GRUB_DISABLE_RECOVERY="true"
```

We want to modify the following line –

```
GRUB_CMDLINE_LINUX="crashkernel=auto rd.lvm.lv=cl/root rd.lvm.lv=cl/swap rhgb quiet"
```

to

```
GRUB_CMDLINE_LINUX="crashkernel=auto rd.lvm.lv=cl/root rd.lvm.lv
=cl/swap rhgb quiet rootflags=usrquota,grpquota"
```

Note – It is important we copy these changes verbatim. After we reconfigure grub.cfg, our system will fail to boot if any errors were made in the configuration. Please, try this part of the tutorial on a non-production system.

Step 3 – Backup your working grub.cfg

```
cp /boot/grub2/grub.cfg /boot/grub2/grub.cfg.bak
```

Make a new grub.cfg

```
[root@localhost rdc]# grub2-mkconfig -o /boot/grub2/grub.cfg
Generating grub configuration file ...
Found linux image: /boot/vmlinuz-3.10.0-514.el7.x86_64
Found initrd image: /boot/initramfs-3.10.0-514.el7.x86_64.img
Found linux image: /boot/vmlinuz-0-rescue-dbba7fa47f73457b96628ba8f3959bfd
Found initrd image: /boot/initramfs-0-rescuedbba7fa47f73457b96628ba8f3959bfd.img
done
[root@localhost rdc]#
```

Reboot

```
[root@localhost rdc]#reboot
```

If all modifications were precise, we should not have the availability to add quotas to the xfs file system.

```
[rdc@localhost ~]$ mount | grep ' / '
/dev/mapper/cl-root on / type xfs (rw,relatime,seclabel,attr2,inode64,usrquota,grpquota)
```

We have passed the usrquota and grpquota parameters via grub.

Now, again edit /etc/fstab to include / since /homeon the same physical disk.

```
/dev/mapper/cl-root/xfs
defaults,usrquota,grpquota       0 0
```

Now let's enable the quota databases.

```
[root@localhost rdc]# quotacheck -acfvugM
```

Make sure Quotas are enabled.

```
[root@localhost rdc]# quotaon -ap
group quota on / (/dev/mapper/cl-root) is on
user quota on / (/dev/mapper/cl-root) is on
group quota on /home (/dev/mapper/cl-home) is on
user quota on /home (/dev/mapper/cl-home) is on
[root@localhost rdc]#
```

Remount the File System

If the partition or disk is separate from the actively booted partition, we can remount without rebooting. If the quota was configured on a disk/partition booted in the root directory /, we may need to reboot the operating system. Forcing the remount and applying changes, the need to remount the filesystem may vary.

```
[rdc@localhost ~]$ df
Filesystem         1K-blocks    Used      Available   Use%    Mounted on
/dev/mapper/cl-root  22447404    4081860  18365544    19%      /
devtmpfs             903448      0        903448      0%       /dev
tmpfs                919308      100      919208      1%       /dev/shm
tmpfs                919308      9180     910128      1%       /run
tmpfs                919308      0        919308      0%       /sys/fs/cgroup
/dev/sda2            1268736     176612   1092124     14%      /boot
/dev/mapper/cl-var   4872192     158024   4714168     4%       /var
/dev/mapper/cl-home  18475008    37284    18437724    1%       /home
tmpfs                183864      8        183856      1%       /run/user/1000
[rdc@localhost ~]$
```

As we can see, LVM volumes are in use. So it's simple to just reboot. This will remount /home and load the /etc/fstab configuration changes into active configuration.

Create Quota Database Files

CentOS is now capable of working with disk quotas on /home. To enable full quota supprt, we must run the quotacheck command.

quotacheck will create two files –

❖ aquota.user
❖ aquota.group

These are used to store quota information for the quota enabled disks/partitions.

Following are the common quotacheck switches.

Switch	Action
-u	Checks for user quotas
-g	Checks for group quotas
-c	Quotas should be enabled for each file system with enables quotas
-v	Displays verbose output

Add Quota Limits Per User

For this, we will use the edquota command, followed by the username –

```
[root@localhost rdc]# edquota centos
Disk quotas for user centos (uid 1000):
Filesystem              blocks    soft    hard    inodes    soft    hard
/dev/mapper/cl-root       12        0       0       13        0       0
/dev/mapper/cl-home      4084       0       0       140       0       0
```

Let's look at each column.

- ❖ Filesystem – It is the filesystem quotas for the user applied to
- ❖ blocks – How many blocks the user is currently using on each filesystem
- ❖ soft – Set blocks for a soft limit. Soft limit allows the user to carry quota for a given time period
- ❖ hard – Set blocks for a hard limit. Hard limit is total allowable quota
- ❖ inodes – How many inodes the user is currently using
- ❖ soft – Soft inode limit
- ❖ hard – Hard inode limit

To check our current quota as a user –

```
[centos@localhost ~]$ quota
Disk quotas for user centos (uid 1000):
Filesystem              blocks    quota    limit grace    files    quota    limit    grace
/dev/mapper/cl-home    6052604  56123456 61234568        475      0        0        [centos@localhost ~]$
```

Following is an error given to a user when the hard quota limit has exceeded.

```
[centos@localhost Downloads]$ cp CentOS-7-x86_64-LiveKDE-1611.iso.part ../Desktop/
cp: cannot create regular file '../Desktop/CentOS-7-x86_64-LiveKDE-
1611.iso.part': Disk quota exceeded
[centos@localhost Downloads]$
```

As we can see, we are closely within this user's disk quota. Let's set a soft limit warning. This way, the user will have advance notice before quota limits expire. From experience, you will get end-user complaints when they come into work and need to spend 45 minutes clearing files to actually get to work.

As an Administrator, we can check quota usage with the repquota command.

```
[root@localhost Downloads]# repquota /home
                Block limits                    File limits
User        used    soft    hard    grace    used    soft    hard    grace
----------------------------------------------------------------------------
root    --     0       0       0              3       0       0
centos  -+  6189824 56123456 61234568        541     520     540     6days
```

As we can see, the user centos has exceeded their hard block quota and can no longer use any more disk space on /home.

-+denotes a hard quota has been exceeded on the filesystem.

When planning quotas, it is necessary to do a little math. What an Administrator needs to know is:How many users are on the system? How much free space to allocate amongst users/groups? How many bytes make up a block on the file system?

Define quotas in terms of blocks as related to free disk-space.It is recommended to leave a "safe" buffer of free-space on the file system that will remain in worst case scenario: all quotas are simultaneously exceeded. This is especially on a partition that is used by the system for writing logs.

SYSTEMD SERVICES START AND STOP

systemd is the new way of running services on Linux. systemd has a superceded sysvinit. systemd brings faster boot-times to Linux and is now, a standard way to manage Linux services. While stable, systemd is still evolving.

systemd as an init system, is used to manage both services and daemons that need status changes after the Linux kernel has been booted. By status change starting, stopping, reloading, and adjusting service state is applied.

First, let's check the version of systemd currently running on our server.

```
[centos@localhost ~]$ systemctl --version
systemd 219
+PAM +AUDIT +SELINUX +IMA -APPARMOR +SMACK +SYSVINIT +UTMP +LIBCRYPTSETUP
+GCRYPT +GNUTLS +ACL    +XZ -LZ4 -SECCOMP +BLKID +ELFUTILS +KMOD +IDN
[centos@localhost ~]$
```

As of CentOS version 7, fully updated at the time of this writing systemd version 219 is the current stable version.

We can also analyze the last server boot time with systemd-analyze

```
[centos@localhost ~]$ systemd-analyze
Startup finished in 1.580s (kernel) + 908ms (initrd) + 53.225s (userspace) = 55.713s
[centos@localhost ~]$
```

When the system boot times are slower, we can use the systemd-analyze blame command.

```
[centos@localhost ~]$ systemd-analyze blame
  40.882s kdump.service
   5.775s NetworkManager-wait-online.service
   4.701s plymouth-quit-wait.service
   3.586s postfix.service
   3.121s systemd-udev-settle.service
   2.649s tuned.service
   1.848s libvirtd.service
   1.437s network.service
   875ms packagekit.service
   855ms gdm.service
   514ms firewalld.service
   438ms rsyslog.service
   436ms udisks2.service
   398ms sshd.service
   360ms boot.mount
   336ms polkit.service
   321ms accounts-daemon.service
```

When working with systemd, it is important to understand the concept of units. Units are the resources systemd knows how to interpret. Units are categorized into 12 types as follows —

- ❖ .service
- ❖ .socket
- ❖ .device
- ❖ .mount
- ❖ .automount

- ❖ .swap
- ❖ .target
- ❖ .path
- ❖ .timer
- ❖ .snapshot
- ❖ .slice
- ❖ .scope

For the most part, we will be working with .service as unit targets. It is recommended to do further research on the other types. As only .service units will apply to starting and stopping systemd services.

Each unit is defined in a file located in either −

- ❖ /lib/systemd/system − base unit files
- ❖ /etc/systemd/system − modified unit files started at run-time

Manage Services with systemctl

To work with systemd, we will need to get very familiar with the systemctl command. Following are the most common command line switches for systemctl.

Switch	Action
-t	Comma separated value of unit types such as service or socket
-a	Shows all loaded units
--state	Shows all units in a defined state, either: load, sub, active, inactive, etc..
-H	Executes operation remotely. Specify Host name or host and user separated by @.

Basic systemctl Usage

```
systemctl [operation]
example: systemctl --state [servicename.service]
```

For a quick look at all the services running on our box.

```
[root@localhost rdc]# systemctl -t service
UNIT              LOAD    ACTIVE   SUB    DESCRIPTION
abrt-ccpp.service       loaded  active  exited   Install ABRT coredump  hook
abrt-oops.service       loaded  active  running  ABRT kernel log watcher
abrt-xorg.service       loaded  active  running  ABRT Xorg log watcher
abrtd.service           loaded  active  running  ABRT Automated Bug Reporting Tool
accounts-daemon.service  loaded  active  running  Accounts Service
alsa-state.service      loaded  active  running  Manage Sound Card State (restore and store)
atd.service          loaded  active  running  Job spooling tools
auditd.service        loaded  active  running  Security Auditing Service
avahi-daemon.service    loaded  active  running  Avahi mDNS/DNS-SD Stack
blk-availability.service  loaded  active  exited   Availability of block devices
bluetooth.service      loaded  active  running  Bluetooth service
chronyd.service        loaded  active  running  NTP client/server
```

Stopping a Service

Let's first, stop the bluetooth service.

```
[root@localhost]# systemctl stop bluetooth
[root@localhost]# systemctl --all -t service | grep bluetooth
bluetooth.service  loaded  inactive dead  Bluetooth service
[root@localhost]#
```

As we can see, the bluetooth service is now inactive.

To start the bluetooth service again.

```
[root@localhost]# systemctl start bluetooth
[root@localhost]# systemctl --all -t service | grep bluetooth
bluetooth.service  loaded  active  running Bluetooth  service
[root@localhost]#
```

Note – We didn't specify bluetooth.service, since the .service is implied. It is a good practice to think of the unit type appending the service we are dealing with. So, from here on, we will use the .service extension to clarify we are working on service unit operations.

The primary actions that can be performed on a service are –

Start	Starts the service
Stop	Stops a service
Reload	Reloads the active configuration of a service w/o stopping it (like kill -HUP in system v init)
Restart	Starts, then stops a service
Enable	Starts a service at boot time
Disable	Stops a service from automatically starting at run time

The above actions are primarily used in the following scenarios –

Start	To bring a service up that has been put in the stopped state.
Stop	To temporarily shut down a service (for example when a service must be stopped to access files locked by the service, as when upgrading the service)
Reload	When a configuration file has been edited and we want to apply the new changes while not stopping the service.
Restart	In the same scenario as reload, but the service does not support reload.
Enable	When we want a disabled service to run at boot time.
Disable	Used primarily when there is a need to stop a service, but it starts on boot.

To check the status of a service –

```
[root@localhost]# systemctl status network.service
network.service - LSB: Bring up/down networking
Loaded: loaded (/etc/rc.d/init.d/network; bad; vendor preset: disabled)
Active: active (exited) since Sat 2017-01-14 04:43:48 EST; 1min 31s ago
Docs: man:systemd-sysv-generator(8)
Process: 923 ExecStart = /etc/rc.d/init.d/network start (code=exited, status = 0/SUCCESS)
localhost.localdomain systemd[1]: Starting LSB: Bring up/down networking...
localhost.localdomain network[923]: Bringing up loopback interface: [ OK ]
localhost.localdomain systemd[1]: Started LSB: Bring up/down networking.
[root@localhost]#
```

Show us the current status of the networking service. If we want to see all the services related to networking, we can use −

```
[root@localhost]# systemctl --all -t service | grep -i network
network.service                  loaded   active   exited   LSB: Bring up/
NetworkManager-wait-online.service   loaded   active   exited   Network Manager
NetworkManager.service               loaded   active   running  Network Manager
ntpd.service                     loaded   inactive dead     Network Time
rhel-import-state.service            loaded   active   exited   Import network
[root@localhost]#
```

For those familiar with the sysinit method of managing services, it is important to make the transition to systemd. systemd is the new way starting and stopping daemon services in Linux.

systemctl is the utility used to control systemd. systemctl provides CentOS administrators with the ability to perform a multitude of operations on systemd including −

- ❖ Configure systemd units
- ❖ Get status of systemd units
- ❖ Start and stop services
- ❖ Enable / disable systemd services for runtime, etc.

The command syntax for systemctl is pretty basic, but can tangle with switches and options. We will present the most essential functions of systemctl needed for administering CentOS Linux.

Basic systemctl syntax:
systemctl [OPTIONS] COMMAND [NAME]

Following are the common commands used with systemctl −

- ❖ start
- ❖ stop
- ❖ restart
- ❖ reload
- ❖ status
- ❖ is-active
- ❖ list-units
- ❖ enable
- ❖ disable
- ❖ cat
- ❖ show

We have already discussed start, stop, reload, restart, enable and disable with systemctl. So let's go over the remaining commonly used commands.

status

In its most simple form, the status command can be used to see the system status as a whole −

```
[root@localhost rdc]# systemctl status
 localhost.localdomain
 State: running
 Jobs: 0 queued
 Failed: 0 units
 Since: Thu 2017-01-19 19:14:37 EST; 4h 5min ago
CGroup: /
        ─1 /usr/lib/systemd/systemd --switched-root --system --deserialize 21
        ─user.slice
          └─user-1002.slice
            └─session-1.scope
              ─2869 gdm-session-worker [pam/gdm-password]
              ─2881 /usr/bin/gnome-keyring-daemon --daemonize --login
```

```
        ├─2888 gnome-session --session gnome-classic
        ├─2895 dbus-launch --sh-syntax --exit-with-session
```

The above output has been condensed. In the real-world systemctl status will output about 100 lines of treed process statuses.

Let's say we want to check the status of our firewall service –

```
[root@localhost rdc]# systemctl status firewalld
● firewalld.service - firewalld - dynamic firewall daemon
Loaded: loaded (/usr/lib/systemd/system/firewalld.service; enabled; vendor preset: enabled)
Active: active (running) since Thu 2017-01-19 19:14:55 EST; 4h 12min ago
  Docs: man:firewalld(1)
Main PID: 825 (firewalld)
CGroup: /system.slice/firewalld.service
        └─825 /usr/bin/python -Es /usr/sbin/firewalld --nofork –nopid
```

As you see, our firewall service is currently active and has been for over 4 hours.

list-units

The list-units command allows us to list all the units of a certain type. Let's check for sockets managed by systemd –

```
[root@localhost]# systemctl list-units --type=socket
UNIT                    LOAD    ACTIVE  SUB         DESCRIPTION
avahi-daemon.socket     loaded  active  running     Avahi mDNS/DNS-SD Stack Activation Socket
cups.socket             loaded  active  running     CUPS Printing Service Sockets
dbus.socket             loaded  active  running     D-Bus System Message Bus Socket
dm-event.socket         loaded  active  listening   Device-mapper event daemon FIFOs
iscsid.socket           loaded  active  listening   Open-iSCSI iscsid Socket
iscsiuio.socket         loaded  active  listening   Open-iSCSI iscsiuio Socket
lvm2-lvmetad.socket     loaded  active  running     LVM2 metadata daemon socket
lvm2-lvmpolld.socket    loaded  active  listening   LVM2 poll daemon socket
rpcbind.socket          loaded  active  listening   RPCbind Server Activation Socket
systemd-initctl.socket  loaded  active  listening   /dev/initctl Compatibility Named Pipe
systemd-journald.socket loaded  active  running     Journal Socket
systemd-shutdownd.socket loaded active  listening   Delayed Shutdown Socket
systemd-udevd-control.socket loaded active running  udev Control Socket
systemd-udevd-kernel.socket loaded active running   udev Kernel Socket
virtlockd.socket        loaded  active  listening   Virtual machine lock manager socket
virtlogd.socket         loaded  active  listening   Virtual machine log manager socket
```

Now let's check the current running services –

```
[root@localhost rdc]# systemctl list-units --type=service
UNIT                    LOAD    ACTIVE  SUB      DESCRIPTION
abrt-ccpp.service       loaded  active  exited   Install ABRT coredump hook
abrt-oops.service       loaded  active  running  ABRT kernel log watcher
abrt-xorg.service       loaded  active  running  ABRT Xorg log watcher
abrtd.service           loaded  active  running  ABRT Automated Bug Reporting Tool
accounts-daemon.service loaded  active  running  Accounts Service
alsa-state.service      loaded  active  running  Manage Sound Card State (restore and store)
atd.service             loaded  active  running  Job spooling tools
auditd.service          loaded  active  running  Security Auditing Service
```

is-active

The is-active command is an example of systemctl commands designed to return the status information of a unit.

```
[root@localhost rdc]# systemctl is-active ksm.service
active
```

cat

cat is one of the seldomly used command. Instead of using cat at the shell and typing the path to a unit file, simply use systemctl cat.

```
[root@localhost]# systemctl cat firewalld
# /usr/lib/systemd/system/firewalld.service
[Unit]
Description=firewalld - dynamic firewall daemon
Before=network.target
Before=libvirtd.service
Before = NetworkManager.service
After=dbus.service
After=polkit.service
Conflicts=iptables.service ip6tables.service ebtables.service ipset.service
Documentation=man:firewalld(1)
[Service]
EnvironmentFile = -/etc/sysconfig/firewalld
ExecStart = /usr/sbin/firewalld --nofork --nopid $FIREWALLD_ARGS
ExecReload = /bin/kill -HUP $MAINPID
# supress to log debug and error output also to /var/log/messages
StandardOutput = null
StandardError = null
Type = dbus
BusName = org.fedoraproject.FirewallD1
[Install]
WantedBy = basic.target
Alias = dbus-org.fedoraproject.FirewallD1.service
[root@localhost]#
```

Now that we have explored both systemd and systemctl in more detail, let's use them to manage the resources in cgroups or control groups.

cgroups or Control Groups are a feature of the Linux kernel that allows an administrator to allocate or cap the system resources for services and also group.

To list active control groups running, we can use the following ps command −

```
[root@localhost]# ps xawf -eo pid,user,cgroup,args
8362 root    -              \_ [kworker/1:2]
1 root       -              /usr/lib/systemd/systemd --switched-
   root --system --  deserialize 21
507 root     7:cpuacct,cpu:/system.slice /usr/lib/systemd/systemd-journald
527 root     7:cpuacct,cpu:/system.slice /usr/sbin/lvmetad -f
540 root     7:cpuacct,cpu:/system.slice /usr/lib/systemd/systemd-udevd
715 root     7:cpuacct,cpu:/system.slice /sbin/auditd -n
731 root     7:cpuacct,cpu:/system.slice \_ /sbin/audispd
734 root     7:cpuacct,cpu:/system.slice \_ /usr/sbin/sedispatch
737 polkitd 7:cpuacct,cpu:/system.slice /usr/lib/polkit-1/polkitd --no-debug
738 rtkit   6:memory:/system.slice/rtki /usr/libexec/rtkit-daemon
740 dbus    7:cpuacct,cpu:/system.slice /bin/dbus-daemon --system --
   address=systemd: --nofork --nopidfile --systemd-activation
```

Resource Management, as of CentOS 6.X, has been redefined with the systemd init implementation. When thinking Resource Management for services, the main thing to focus on are cgroups. cgroups have advanced with systemd in both functionality and simplicity.

The goal of cgroups in resource management is -no one service can take the system, as a whole, down. Or no single service process (perhaps a poorly written PHP script) will cripple the server functionality by consuming too many resources.

cgroups allow resource control of units for the following resources −

❖ CPU − Limit cpu intensive tasks that are not critical as other, less intensive tasks
❖ Memory − Limit how much memory a service can consume
❖ Disks − Limit disk i/o

**CPU Time: **

Tasks needing less CPU priority can have custom configured CPU Slices.

Let's take a look at the following two services for example.

Polite CPU Service 1

```
[root@localhost]# systemctl cat polite.service
# /etc/systemd/system/polite.service
[Unit]
Description = Polite service limits CPU Slice and Memory
After=remote-fs.target nss-lookup.target
[Service]
MemoryLimit = 1M
ExecStart = /usr/bin/sha1sum /dev/zero
ExecStop = /bin/kill -WINCH ${MAINPID}
WantedBy=multi-user.target
# /etc/systemd/system/polite.service.d/50-CPUShares.conf
[Service]
```

```
CPUShares = 1024
[root@localhost]#
```

Evil CPU Service 2

```
[root@localhost]# systemctl cat evil.service
# /etc/systemd/system/evil.service
[Unit]
Description = I Eat You CPU
After=remote-fs.target nss-lookup.target
[Service]
ExecStart = /usr/bin/md5sum /dev/zero
ExecStop = /bin/kill -WINCH ${MAINPID}
WantedBy=multi-user.target
# /etc/systemd/system/evil.service.d/50-CPUShares.conf
[Service]
CPUShares = 1024
[root@localhost]#
```

Let's set Polite Service using a lesser CPU priority −

```
systemctl set-property polite.service CPUShares = 20
/system.slice/polite.service
1  70.5  124.0K    -    -
/system.slice/evil.service
1  99.5  304.0K    -    -
```

As we can see, over a period of normal system idle time, both rogue processes are still using CPU cycles. However, the one set to have less time-slices is using less CPU time. With this in mind, we can see how using a lesser time time-slice would allow essential tasks better access the system resources.

To set services for each resource, the set-property method defines the following parameters −

```
systemctl set-property name parameter=value
```

CPU Slices	CPUShares
Memory Limit	MemoryLimit
Soft Memory Limit	MemorySoftLimit
Block IO Weight	BlockIOWeight
Block Device Limit (specified in /volume/path))	BlockIODeviceWeight
Read IO	BlockIOReadBandwidth
Disk Write IO	BlockIOReadBandwidth

Most often services will be limited by CPU use, Memory limits and Read / Write IO.

After changing each, it is necessary to reload systemd and restart the service −

```
systemctl set-property foo.service CPUShares = 250
systemctl daemon-reload
systemctl restart foo.service
```

Configure CGroups in CentOS Linux

To make custom cgroups in CentOS Linux, we need to first install services and configure them.

Step 1 − Install libcgroup (if not already installed).

```
[root@localhost]# yum install libcgroup
Package libcgroup-0.41-11.el7.x86_64 already installed and latest version
Nothing to do
[root@localhost]#
```

As we can see, by default CentOS 7 has libcgroup installed with the everything installer. Using a minimal installer will require us to install the libcgroup utilities along with any dependencies.

Step 2 − Start and enable the cgconfig service.

```
[root@localhost]# systemctl enable cgconfig
Created symlink from /etc/systemd/system/sysinit.target.wants/cgconfig.service to
/usr/lib/systemd/system/cgconfig.service.
[root@localhost]# systemctl start cgconfig
[root@localhost]# systemctl status cgconfig
cgconfig.service - Control Group configuration service
Loaded: loaded (/usr/lib/systemd/system/cgconfig.service; enabled; vendor preset: disabled)
Active: active (exited) since Mon 2017-01-23 02:51:42 EST; 1min 21s ago
Main PID: 4692 (code=exited, status = 0/SUCCESS)
Memory: 0B
CGroup: /system.slice/cgconfig.service
Jan 23 02:51:42 localhost.localdomain systemd[1]: Starting Control Group configuration service...
Jan 23 02:51:42 localhost.localdomain systemd[1]: Started Control Group configuration service.
[root@localhost]#
```

LINUX ADMIN - PROCESS MANAGEMENT

Following are the common commands used with Process Management–bg, fg, nohup, ps, pstree, top, kill, killall, free, uptime, nice.

Work with Processes

Quick Note: Process PID in Linux

In Linux every running process is given a PID or Process ID Number. This PID is how CentOS identifies a particular process. As we have discussed, systemd is the first process started and given a PID of 1 in CentOS.

Pgrep is used to get Linux PID for a given process name.

```
[root@CentOS]# pgrep systemd
1
```

As seen, the pgrep command returns the current PID of systemd.

Basic CentOS Process and Job Management in CentOS

When working with processes in Linux it is important to know how basic foregrounding and backgrounding processes is performed at the command line.

- ❖ fg – Bringsthe process to the foreground
- ❖ bg – Movesthe process to the background
- ❖ jobs – List of the current processes attached to the shell
- ❖ ctrl+z – Control + z key combination to sleep the current process
- ❖ & – Startsthe process in the background

Let's start using the shell command sleep. sleep will simply do as it is named, sleep for a defined period of time: sleep.

```
[root@CentOS ~]$ jobs
[root@CentOS ~]$ sleep 10 &
[1] 12454
[root@CentOS ~]$ sleep 20 &
[2] 12479
[root@CentOS ~]$ jobs
[1]- Running          sleep 10 &
[2]+ Running          sleep 20 &
[cnetos@CentOS ~]$
```

Now, let's bring the first job to the foreground –

```
[root@CentOS ~]$ fg 1
sleep 10
```

If you are following along, you'll notice the foreground job is stuck in your shell. Now, let's put the process to sleep, then re-enable it in the background.

- ❖ Hit control+z
- ❖ Type: bg 1, sending the first job into the background and starting it.

```
[root@CentOS ~]$ fg 1
sleep 20
^Z
[1]+ Stopped          sleep 20
[root@CentOS ~]$ bg 1
[1]+ sleep 20 &
[root@CentOS ~]$
```

nohup

When working from a shell or terminal, it is worth noting that by default all the processes and jobs attached to the shell will terminate when the shell is closed or the user logs out. When using nohup the process will continue to run if the user logs out or closes the shell to which the process is attached.

```
[root@CentOS]# nohup ping www.google.com &
[1] 27299
nohup: ignoring input and appending output to 'nohup.out'
[root@CentOS]# pgrep ping
27299
[root@CentOS]# kill -KILL `pgrep ping`
[1]+ Killed              nohup ping www.google.com
[root@CentOS rdc]# cat nohup.out
PING www.google.com (216.58.193.68) 56(84) bytes of data.
64 bytes from sea15s07-in-f4.1e100.net (216.58.193.68): icmp_seq = 1 ttl = 128
time = 51.6 ms
64 bytes from sea15s07-in-f4.1e100.net (216.58.193.68): icmp_seq = 2 ttl = 128
time = 54.2 ms
64 bytes from sea15s07-in-f4.1e100.net (216.58.193.68): icmp_seq = 3 ttl = 128
time = 52.7 ms
```

ps Command

The ps command is commonly used by administrators to investigate snapshots of a specific process. ps is commonly used with grep to filter out a specific process to analyze.

```
[root@CentOS ~]$ ps axw | grep python
762  ?     Ssl  0:01 /usr/bin/python -Es /usr/sbin/firewalld --nofork -nopid
1296 ?     Ssl  0:00 /usr/bin/python -Es /usr/sbin/tuned -l -P
15550 pts/0  S+   0:00 grep --color=auto python
```

In the above command, we see all the processes using the python interpreter. Also included with the results were our grep command, looking for the string python.

Following are the most common command line switches used with ps.

Switch	Action
a	Excludes constraints of only the reporting processes for the current user
x	Shows processes not attached to a tty or shell
w	Formats wide output display of the output
e	Shows environment after the command
-e	Selects all processes
-o	User-defined formatted output

-u	Shows all processes by a specific user
-C	Shows all processes by name or process id
--sort	Sorts the processes by definition

To see all processes in use by the nobody user –

```
[root@CentOS ~]$ ps -u nobody
PID TTY      TIME CMD
1853 ?     00:00:00 dnsmasq
[root@CentOS ~]$
```

To see all information about the firewalld process –

```
[root@CentOS ~]$ ps -wl -C firewalld
F  S  UID  PID  PPID  C  PRI  NI  ADDR  SZ  WCHAN  TTY  TIME     CMD
0  S  0  762   1  0  80  0  -  81786  poll_s  ?  00:00:01 firewalld
[root@CentOS ~]$
```

Let's see which processes are consuming the most memory –

```
[root@CentOS ~]$ ps aux --sort=-pmem | head -10
USER    PID  %CPU  %MEM  VSZ    RSS  TTY  STAT  START  TIME  COMMAND
cnetos   6130  0.7  5.7  1344512 108364  ?     Sl  02:16  0:29  /usr/bin/gnome-shell
cnetos   6449  0.0  3.4  1375872 64440   ?     Sl  02:16  0:00  /usr/libexec/evolution-calendar-factory
root     5404  0.6  2.1  190256 39920 tty1    Ssl+ 02:15  0:27  /usr/bin/Xorg :0 -background none -noreset -audit 4
-verbose -auth /run/gdm/auth-for-gdm-iDefCt/database -seat seat0 -nolisten tcp vt1
cnetos   6296  0.0  1.7  1081944 32136  ?     Sl  02:16  0:00  /usr/libexec/evolution/3.12/evolution-alarm-notify
cnetos   6350  0.0  1.5  560728 29844  ?     Sl  02:16  0:01  /usr/bin/prlsga
cnetos   6158  0.0  1.4  1026956 28004  ?     Sl  02:16  0:00  /usr/libexec/gnome-shell-calendar-server
cnetos   6169  0.0  1.4  1120028 27576  ?     Sl  02:16  0:00  /usr/libexec/evolution-source-registry
root      762  0.0  1.4  327144 26724  ?     Ssl 02:09  0:01  /usr/bin/python -Es /usr/sbin/firewalld --nofork --
nopid
cnetos   6026  0.0  1.4  1090832 26376    ?   Sl  02:16  0:00  /usr/libexec/gnome-settings-daemon
[root@CentOS ~]$
```

See all the processes by user centos and format, displaying the custom output –

```
[cnetos@CentOS ~]$ ps -u cnetos -o pid,uname,comm
 PID   USER   COMMAND
5802  centos  gnome-keyring-d
5812  cnetos  gnome-session
5819  cnetos  dbus-launch
5820  cnetos  dbus-daemon
5888  cnetos  gvfsd
5893  cnetos  gvfsd-fuse
5980  cnetos  ssh-agent
5996  cnetos  at-spi-bus-laun
```

pstree Command

pstree is similar to ps but is not often used. It displays the processes in a neater tree fashion.

```
[centos@CentOS ~]$ pstree
systemd─┬─ModemManager───────2*[{ModemManager}]
        ├─NetworkManager─┬─dhclient
        │                └─2*[{NetworkManager}]
        ├─2*[abrt-watch-log]
        ├─abrtd
        ├─accounts-daemon──────2*[{accounts-daemon}]
        ├─alsactl
        ├─at-spi-bus-laun─┬─dbus-daemon──────{dbus-daemon}
        │                 └─3*[{at-spi-bus-laun}]
```

```
    ─at-spi2-registr──────2*[{at-spi2-registr}]
    ─atd
    ─auditd──┬─auditspd──┬─sedispatch
    │        │           └─{auditspd}
    │        └─{auditd}
    ─avahi-daemon──────avahi-daemon
    ─caribou──────2*[{caribou}]
    ─cgrulesengd
    ─chronyd
    ─colord──────2*[{colord}]
    ─crond
    ─cupsd
```

The total output from pstree can exceed 100 lines. Usually, ps will give more useful information.

top Command

top is one of the most often used commands when troubleshooting performance issues in Linux. It is useful for real-time stats and process monitoring in Linux. Following is the default output of top when brought up from the command line.

```
Tasks: 170 total,  1 running, 169 sleeping,  0 stopped,  0 zombie
%Cpu(s): 2.3 us,  2.0 sy,  0.0 ni, 95.7 id,  0.0 wa,  0.0 hi,  0.0 si,  0.0 st
KiB Mem : 1879668 total,  177020 free,  607544 used, 1095104 buff/cache
KiB Swap: 3145724 total, 3145428 free,     296 used. 1034648 avail Mem

PID   USER    PR  NI  VIRT    RES   SHR  S %CPU %MEM TIME+   COMMAND
5404  root    20  0   197832  48024 6744 S 1.3  2.6  1:13.22 Xorg
8013  centos  20  0   555316  23104 13140 S 1.0  1.2  0:14.89 gnome-terminal-
6339  centos  20  0   332336  6016  3248 S 0.3  0.3  0:23.71 prlcc
6351  centos  20  0   21044   1532  1292 S 0.3  0.1  0:02.66 prlshprof
```

Common hot keys used while running top (hot keys are accessed by pressing the key as top is running in your shell).

Command	Action
b	Enables / disables bold highlighting on top menu
z	Cycles the color scheme
l	Cycles the load average heading
m	Cycles the memory average heading
t	Task information heading
h	Help menu
Shift+F	Customizes sorting and display fields

Following are the common command line switches for top.

Command	Action
-o	Sorts by column (can prepend with - or + to sort ascending or descending)
-u	Shows only processes from a specified user
-d	Updates the delay time of top
-O	Returns a list of columns which top can apply sorting

Sorting options screen in top, presented using Shift+F. This screen allows customization of top display and sort options.

Fields Management for window 1:Def, whose current sort field is %MEM
Navigate with Up/Dn, Right selects for move then <Enter> or Left commits,
'd' or <Space> toggles display, 's' sets sort. Use 'q' or <Esc> to end!

```
* PID     = Process Id         TGID   = Thread Group Id
* USER    = Effective User Name  ENVIRON = Environment vars
* PR      = Priority           vMj    = Major Faults delta
* NI      = Nice Value         vMn    = Minor Faults delta
* VIRT    = Virtual Image (KiB)  USED   = Res+Swap Size (KiB)
* RES     = Resident Size (KiB)  nsIPC  = IPC namespace Inode
* SHR     = Shared Memory (KiB)  nsMNT  = MNT namespace Inode
* S       = Process Status      nsNET  = NET namespace Inode
* %CPU    = CPU Usage           nsPID  = PID namespace Inode
* %MEM    = Memory Usage (RES)   nsUSER = USER namespace Inode
* TIME+   = CPU Time, hundredths nsUTS  = UTS namespace Inode
* COMMAND = Command Name/Line
  PPID    = Parent Process pid
  UID     = Effective User Id
```

top, showing the processes for user rdc and sorted by memory usage −

PID	USER	%MEM	PR	NI	VIRT	RES	SHR	S	%CPU	TIME+	COMMAND
6130	rdc	6.2	20	0	1349592	117160	33232	S	0.0	1:09.34	gnome-shell
6449	rdc	3.4	20	0	1375872	64428	21400	S	0.0	0:00.43	evolution-calen
6296	rdc	1.7	20	0	1081944	32140	22596	S	0.0	0:00.40	evolution-alarm
6350	rdc	1.6	20	0	560728	29844	4256	S	0.0	0:10.16	prlsga
6281	rdc	1.5	20	0	1027176	28808	17680	S	0.0	0:00.78	nautilus
6158	rdc	1.5	20	0	1026956	28004	19072	S	0.0	0:00.20	gnome-shell-cal

Showing valid top fields (condensed) −

```
[centos@CentOS ~]$ top -O
PID
PPID
UID
USER
RUID
RUSER
SUID
SUSER
GID
GROUP
PGRP
TTY
TPGID
```

kill Command

The kill command is used to kill a process from the command shell via its PID.
When killing a process, we need to specify a signal to send. The signal lets the
kernel know how we want to end the process. The most commonly used signals
are −

- ❖ SIGTERM is implied as the kernel lets a process know it should stop
  soon as it is safe to do so. SIGTERM gives the process an opportunity to
  exit gracefully and perform safe exit operations.
- ❖ SIGHUP most daemons will restart when sent SIGHUP. This is often
  used on the processes when changes have been made to a configuration
  file.

- ❖ SIGKILL since SIGTERM is the equivalent to asking a process to shut down. The kernel needs an option to end a process that will not comply with requests. When a process is hung, the SIGKILL option is used to shut the process down explicitly.

For a list off all signals that can be sent with kill the -l option can be used −

```
[root@CentOS]# kill -l
 1) SIGHUP       2) SIGINT       3) SIGQUIT      4) SIGILL       5) SIGTRAP
 6) SIGABRT      7) SIGBUS       8) SIGFPE       9) SIGKILL     10) SIGUSR1
11) SIGSEGV     12) SIGUSR2     13) SIGPIPE     14) SIGALRM     15) SIGTERM
16) SIGSTKFLT   17) SIGCHLD     18) SIGCONT     19) SIGSTOP     20) SIGTSTP
21) SIGTTIN     22) SIGTTOU     23) SIGURG      24) SIGXCPU     25) SIGXFSZ
26) SIGVTALRM   27) SIGPROF     28) SIGWINCH    29) SIGIO       30) SIGPWR
31) SIGSYS      34) SIGRTMIN    35) SIGRTMIN+1  36) SIGRTMIN+2  37) SIGRTMIN+3
38) SIGRTMIN+4  39) SIGRTMIN+5  40) SIGRTMIN+6  41) SIGRTMIN+7  42) SIGRTMIN+8
43) SIGRTMIN+9  44) SIGRTMIN+10 45) SIGRTMIN+11 46) SIGRTMIN+12 47) SIGRTMIN+13
48) SIGRTMIN+14 49) SIGRTMIN+15 50) SIGRTMAX-14 51) SIGRTMAX-13 52) SIGRTMAX-12
53) SIGRTMAX-11 54) SIGRTMAX-10 55) SIGRTMAX-9  56) SIGRTMAX-8  57) SIGRTMAX-7
58) SIGRTMAX-6  59) SIGRTMAX-5  60) SIGRTMAX-4  61) SIGRTMAX-3  62) SIGRTMAX-2
63) SIGRTMAX-1  64) SIGRTMAX
[root@CentOS rdc]#
```

Using SIGHUP to restart system.

```
[root@CentOS]# pgrep systemd
1
464
500
643
15071
[root@CentOS]# kill -HUP 1
[root@CentOS]# pgrep systemd
1
464
500
643
15196
15197
15198
[root@CentOS]#
```

pkill will allow the administrator to send a kill signal by the process name.

```
[root@CentOS]# pgrep ping
19450
[root@CentOS]# pkill -9 ping
[root@CentOS]# pgrep ping
```

killall will kill all the processes. Be careful using killall as root, as it will kill all the processes for all users.

```
[root@CentOS]# killall chrome
```

free Command

free is a pretty simple command often used to quickly check the memory of a system. It displays the total amount of used physical and swap memory.

```
[root@CentOS]# free
          total    used    free    shared    buff/cache    available
```

| Mem: | 1879668 | 526284 | 699796 | 10304 | 653588 | 1141412 |
| Swap: | 3145724 | 0 | 3145724 | | | |

[root@CentOS]#

nice Command

nice will allow an administrator to set the scheduling priority of a process in terms of CPU usages. The niceness is basically how the kernel will schedule CPU time slices for a process or job. By default, it is assumed the process is given equal access to CPU resources.

First, let's use top to check the niceness of the currently running processes.

PID	USER	PR	NI	VIRT	RES	SHR	S	%CPU	%MEM	TIME+	COMMAND
28	root	39	19	0	0	0	S	0.0	0.0	0:00.17	khugepaged
690	root	39	19	16808	1396	1164	S	0.0	0.1	0:00.01	alsactl]
9598	rdc	39	19	980596	21904	10284	S	0.0	1.2	0:00.27	tracker-extract
9599	rdc	39	19	469876	9608	6980	S	0.0	0.5	0:00.04	tracker-miner-a
9609	rdc	39	19	636528	13172	8044	S	0.0	0.7	0:00.12	tracker-miner-f
9611	rdc	39	19	469620	8984	6496	S	0.0	0.5	0:00.02	tracker-miner-u
27	root	25	5	0	0	0	S	0.0	0.0	0:00.00	ksmd
637	rtkit	21	1	164648	1276	1068	S	0.0	0.1	0:00.11	rtkit-daemon
1	root	20	0	128096	6712	3964	S	0.3	0.4	0:03.57	systemd
2	root	20	0	0	0	0	S	0.0	0.0	0:00.01	kthreadd
3	root	20	0	0	0	0	S	0.0	0.0	0:00.50	ksofirqd/0
7	root	20	0	0	0	0	S	0.0	0.0	0:00.00	migration/0
8	root	20	0	0	0	0	S	0.0	0.0	0:00.00	rcu_bh
9	root	20	0	0	0	0	S	0.0	0.0	0:02.07	rcu_sched

We want to focus on the NICE column depicted by NI. The niceness range can be anywhere between -20 to positive 19. -20 represents the highest given priority.

nohup nice --20 ping www.google.com &

renice

renice allows us to change the current priority of a process that is already running.

renice 17 -p 30727

The above command will lower the priority of our ping process command.

LINUX ADMIN - FIREWALL SETUP

firewalld is the default front-end controller for iptables on CentOS. The firewalld front-end has two main advantages over raw iptables −

* ❖ Uses easy-to-configure and implement zones abstracting chains and rules.
* ❖ Rulesets are dynamic, meaning stateful connections are uninterrupted when the settings are changed and/or modified.

Remember, firewalld is the wrapper for iptables - not a replacement. While custom iptables commands can be used with firewalld, it is recommended to use firewalld as to not break the firewall functionality.

First, let's make sure firewalld is both started and enabled.

```
[root@CentOS rdc]# systemctl status firewalld
● firewalld.service - firewalld - dynamic firewall daemon
Loaded: loaded (/usr/lib/systemd/system/firewalld.service; enabled; vendor preset: enabled)
Active: active (running) since Thu 2017-01-26 21:42:05 MST; 3h 46min ago
Docs: man:firewalld(1)
Main PID: 712 (firewalld)
 Memory: 34.7M
CGroup: /system.slice/firewalld.service
    └─712 /usr/bin/python -Es /usr/sbin/firewalld --nofork --nopid
```

We can see, firewalld is both active (to start on boot) and currently running. If inactive or not started we can use −

```
systemctl start firewalld && systemctl enable firewalld
```

Now that we have our firewalld service configured, let's assure it is operational.

```
[root@CentOS]# firewall-cmd --state
running
[root@CentOS]#
```

We can see, the firewalld service is fully functional.

Firewalld works on the concept of zones. A zone is applied to network interfaces through the Network Manager. We will discuss this in configuring networking. But for now, by default, changing the default zone will change any network adapters left in the default state of "Default Zone".

Let's take a quick look at each zone that comes out-of-the-box with firewalld.

Sr.No.	Zone & Description
1	drop Low trust level. All incoming connections and packetsare dropped and only outgoing connections are possible via statefullness
2	block Incoming connections are replied with an icmp message letting the initiator know the request is prohibited
3	public All networks are restricted. However, selected incoming connections can be explicitly allowed

4	external
	Configures firewalld for NAT. Internal network remains private but reachable
5	dmz
	Only certain incoming connections are allowed. Used for systems in DMZ isolation
6	work
	By default, trust more computers on the network assuming the system is in a secured work environment
7	hone
	By default, more services are unfiltered. Assuming a system is on a home network where services such as NFS, SAMBA and SSDP will be used
8	trusted
	All machines on the network are trusted. Most incoming connections are allowed unfettered. This is not meant for interfaces exposed to the Internet

The most common zones to use are:public, drop, work, and home.

Some scenarios where each common zone would be used are −

- ❖ public − It is the most common zone used by an administrator. It will let you apply the custom settings and abide by RFC specifications for operations on a LAN.
- ❖ drop − A good example of when to use drop is at a security conference, on public WiFi, or on an interface connected directly to the Internet. drop assumes all unsolicited requests are malicious including ICMP probes. So any request out of state will not receive a reply. The downside of drop is that it can break the functionality of applications in certain situations requiring strict RFC compliance.
- ❖ work − You are on a semi-secure corporate LAN. Where all traffic can be assumed moderately safe. This means it is not WiFi and we possibly have IDS, IPS, and physical security or 802.1x in place. We also should be familiar with the people using the LAN.
- ❖ home − You are on a home LAN. You are personally accountable for every system and the user on the LAN. You know every machine on the LAN and that none have been compromised. Often new services are brought up for media sharing amongst trusted individuals and you don't need to take extra time for the sake of security.

Zones and network interfaces work on a one to many level. One network interface can only have a single zone applied to it at a time. While, a zone can be applied to many interfaces simultaneously.

Let's see what zones are available and what are the currently applied zone.

```
[root@CentOS]# firewall-cmd --get-zones
 work drop internal external trusted home dmz public block
[root@CentOS]# firewall-cmd --get-default-zone
public
[root@CentOS]#
```

Ready to add some customized rules in firewalld?

First, let's see what our box looks like, to a portscanner from outside.

```
bash-3.2# nmap -sS -p 1-1024 -T 5  10.211.55.1

Starting Nmap 7.30 ( https://nmap.org ) at 2017-01-27 23:36 MST
Nmap scan report for centos.shared (10.211.55.1)
Host is up (0.00046s latency).
Not shown: 1023 filtered ports
PORT   STATE SERVICE
22/tcp open  ssh

Nmap done: 1 IP address (1 host up) scanned in 3.71 seconds
bash-3.2#
```

Let's allow the incoming requests to port 80.

First, check to see what zone is applied as default.

```
[root@CentOs]# firewall-cmd --get-default-zone
public
[root@CentOS]#
```

Then, set the rule allowing port 80 to the current default zone.

```
[root@CentOS]# firewall-cmd --zone=public --add-port = 80/tcp
success
[root@CentOS]#
```

Now, let's check our box after allowing port 80 connections.

```
bash-3.2# nmap -sS -p 1-1024 -T 5  10.211.55.1
Starting Nmap 7.30 ( https://nmap.org ) at 2017-01-27 23:42 MST
Nmap scan report for centos.shared (10.211.55.1)
Host is up (0.00053s latency).
Not shown: 1022 filtered ports
PORT   STATE SERVICE
22/tcp open   ssh
80/tcp closed http
Nmap done: 1 IP address (1 host up) scanned in 3.67 seconds
bash-3.2#
```

It now allows unsolicited traffic to 80.

Let's put the default zone to drop and see what happens to port scan.

```
[root@CentOS]# firewall-cmd --set-default-zone=drop
success
[root@CentOS]# firewall-cmd --get-default-zone
drop
[root@CentOs]#
```

Now let's scan the host with the network interface in a more secure zone.

```
bash-3.2# nmap -sS -p 1-1024 -T 5  10.211.55.1
Starting Nmap 7.30 ( https://nmap.org ) at 2017-01-27 23:50 MST
Nmap scan report for centos.shared (10.211.55.1)
Host is up (0.00094s latency).
All 1024 scanned ports on centos.shared (10.211.55.1) are filtered
Nmap done: 1 IP address (1 host up) scanned in 12.61 seconds
bash-3.2#
```

Now, everything is filtered from outside.

As demonstrated below, the host will not even respond to ICMP ping requests when in drop.

```
bash-3.2# ping 10.211.55.1
PING 10.211.55.1 (10.211.55.1): 56 data bytes
Request timeout for icmp_seq 0
Request timeout for icmp_seq 1
Request timeout for icmp_seq 2
```

Let's set the default zone to public again.

```
[root@CentOs]# firewall-cmd --set-default-zone=public
success
[root@CentOS]# firewall-cmd --get-default-zone
public
[root@CentOS]#
```

Now let's check our current filtering ruleset in public.

```
[root@CentOS]# firewall-cmd --zone=public --list-all
public (active)
target: default
icmp-block-inversion: no
interfaces: enp0s5
sources:
services: dhcpv6-client ssh
ports: 80/tcp
protocols:
masquerade: no
forward-ports:
sourceports:
icmp-blocks:
rich rules:
[root@CentOS rdc]#
```

As configured, our port 80 filter rule is only within the context of the running configuration. This means once the system is rebooted or the firewalld service is restarted, our rule will be discarded.

We will be configuring an httpd daemon soon, so let's make our changes persistent −

```
[root@CentOS]# firewall-cmd --zone=public --add-port=80/tcp --permanent
success
[root@CentOS]# systemctl restart firewalld
[root@CentOS]#
```

Now our port 80 rule in the public zone is persistent across reboots and service restarts.

Following are the common firewalld commands applied with firewall-cmd.

Command	Action
firewall-cmd --get-zones	Lists all zones that can be applied to an interface
firewall-cmd —status	Returns the currents status of the firewalld service
firewall-cmd --get-default-zone	Gets the current default zone
firewall-cmd --set-default-zone=<zone>	Sets the default zone into the current context
firewall-cmd --get-active-zone	Gets the current zones in context as applied to an interface

firewall-cmd --zone=<zone> --list-all	Lists the configuration of supplied zone
firewall-cmd --zone=<zone> --addport=<port/transport protocol>	Applies a port rule to the zone filter
--permanent	Makes changes to the zone persistent. Flag is used inline with modification commands

These are the basic concepts of administrating and configuring firewalld.

Configuring host-based firewall services in CentOS can be a complex task in more sophisticated networking scenarios. Advanced usage and configuration of firewalld and iptables in CentOS can take an entire tutorial. However, we have presented the basics that should be enough to complete a majority of daily tasks.

CONFIGURE PHP IN CENTOS LINUX

PHP is the one of the most prolific web languages in use today. Installing a LAMP Stack on CentOS is something every system administrator will need to perform, most likely sooner than later.

A traditional LAMP Stack consists of (L)inux (A)pache (M)ySQL (P)HP.

There are three main components to a LAMP Stack on CentOS –

- ❖ Web Server
- ❖ Web Development Platform / Language
- ❖ Database Server

Note – The term LAMP Stack can also include the following technologies: PostgreSQL, MariaDB, Perl, Python, Ruby, NGINX Webserver.

For this tutorial, we will stick with the traditional LAMP Stack of CentOS GNU Linux: Apache web server, MySQL Database Server, and PHP.

We will actually be using MariaDB. MySQL configuration files, databases and tables are transparent to MariaDB. MariaDB is now included in the standard CentOS repository instead of MySQL. This is due to the limitations of licensing and open-source compliance, since Oracle has taken over the development of MySQL.

The first thing we need to do is install Apache.

```
[root@CentOS]# yum install httpd
Loaded plugins: fastestmirror, langpacks
base
| 3.6 kB  00:00:00
extras
| 3.4 kB  00:00:00
updates
| 3.4 kB  00:00:00
extras/7/x86_64/primary_d
| 121 kB  00:00:00
Loading mirror speeds from cached hostfile
* base: mirror.sigmanet.com
* extras: linux.mirrors.es.net
* updates: mirror.eboundhost.com
Resolving Dependencies
--> Running transaction check
---> Package httpd.x86_64 0:2.4.6-45.el7.centos will be installed
--> Processing Dependency: httpd-tools = 2.4.6-45.el7.centos for package:
httpd-2.4.6-45.el7.centos.x86_64
--> Processing Dependency: /etc/mime.types for package: httpd-2.4.645.el7.centos.x86_64
--> Running transaction check
---> Package httpd-tools.x86_64 0:2.4.6-45.el7.centos will be installed
---> Package mailcap.noarch 0:2.1.41-2.el7 will be installed
--> Finished Dependency Resolution
Installed:
httpd.x86_64 0:2.4.6-45.el7.centos
Dependency Installed:
httpd-tools.x86_64 0:2.4.6-45.el7.centos
mailcap.noarch 0:2.1.41-2.el7
Complete!
[root@CentOS]#
```

Let's configure httpd service.

```
[root@CentOS]# systemctl start httpd && systemctl enable httpd
```

Now, let's make sure the web-server is accessible through firewalld.

```
bash-3.2# nmap -sS -p 1-1024 -T 5 -sV 10.211.55.1
Starting Nmap 7.30 ( https://nmap.org ) at 2017-01-28 02:00 MST
Nmap scan report for centos.shared (10.211.55.1)
Host is up (0.00054s latency).
Not shown: 1022 filtered ports
PORT    STATE SERVICE VERSION
22/tcp open  ssh     OpenSSH 6.6.1 (protocol 2.0)
80/tcp open  http    Apache httpd 2.4.6 ((CentOS))
Service detection performed. Please report any incorrect results at
https://nmap.org/submit/ .
Nmap done: 1 IP address (1 host up) scanned in 10.82 seconds bash-3.2#
```

As you can see by the nmap service probe, Apache webserver is listening and responding to requests on the CentOS host.

Install MySQL Database Server

```
[root@CentOS rdc]# yum install mariadb-server.x86_64 && yum install mariadb-
devel.x86_64 && mariadb.x86_64 && mariadb-libs.x86_64
```

We are installing the following repository packages for MariaDB −

mariadb-server.x86_64

The main MariaDB Server daemon package.

mariadb-devel.x86_64

Files need to compile from the source with MySQL/MariaDB compatibility.

mariadb.x86_64

MariaDB client utilities for administering MariaDB Server from the command line.

mariadb-libs.x86_64

Common libraries for MariaDB that could be needed for other applications compiled with MySQL/MariaDB support.

Now, let's start and enable the MariaDB Service.

```
[root@CentOS]# systemctl start mariadb
[root@CentOS]# systemctl enable  mariadb
```

Note − Unlike Apache, we will not enable connections to MariaDB through our host-based firewall (firewalld). When using a database server, it's considered best security practice to only allow local socket connections, unless the remote socket access is specifically needed.

Let's make sure the MariaDB Server is accepting connections.

```
[root@CentOS#] netstat -lnt
Active Internet connections (only servers)
Proto   Recv-Q   Send-Q   Local Address        Foreign Address   State
tcp     0        0        0.0.0.0:3306         0.0.0.0:*         LISTEN
tcp     0        0        0.0.0.0:111          0.0.0.0:*         LISTEN
tcp     0        0        192.168.122.1:53     0.0.0.0:*         LISTEN
tcp     0        0        0.0.0.0:22           0.0.0.0:*         LISTEN
tcp     0        0        127.0.0.1:631        0.0.0.0:*         LISTEN
tcp     0        0        127.0.0.1:25         0.0.0.0:*         LISTEN

[root@CentOS rdc]#
```

As we can see, MariaDB is listening on port 3306 tcp. We will leave our host-based firewall (firewalld) blocking incoming connections to port 3306.

Install and Configure PHP

```
[root@CentOS#]  yum install php.x86_64 && php-common.x86_64 && php-mysql.x86_64
&& php-mysqlnd.x86_64 && php-pdo.x86_64 && php-soap.x86_64 && php-xml.x86_64
```

I'd recommend installing the following php packages for common compatibility –

- ❖   php-common.x86_64
- ❖   php-mysql.x86_64
- ❖   php-mysqlnd.x86_64
- ❖   php-pdo.x86_64
- ❖   php-soap.x86_64
- ❖   php-xml.x86_64

```
[root@CentOS]# yum install -y php-common.x86_64 php-mysql.x86_64 php-
mysqlnd.x86_64 php-pdo.x86_64 php-soap.x86_64 php-xml.x86_64
```

This is our simple php file located in the Apache webroot of /var/www/html/

```
[root@CentOS]# cat /var/www/html/index.php
<html>
  <head>
   <title>PHP Test Page</title>
  </head>

  <body>
   PHP Install
   <?php
     echo "We are now running PHP on GNU Centos Linux!<br />"
   ?>
  </body>
</html>
[root@CentOS]#
```

Let's change the owning group of our page to the system user our http daemon is running under.

```
[root@CentOS]# chgrp httpd /var/www/html/index.php && chmod g+rx /var/www/html/index.php
---
```

When requested manually via ncat.

```
bash-3.2# ncat 10.211.55.1 80
```

```
GET / index.php
HTTP/1.1 200 OK
Date: Sat, 28 Jan 2017 12:06:02 GMT
Server: Apache/2.4.6 (CentOS) PHP/5.4.16
X-Powered-By: PHP/5.4.16
Content-Length: 137
Connection: close
Content-Type: text/html; charset=UTF-8

<html>
  <head>
    <title>PHP Test Page</title>
  </head>

  <body>
    PHP Install
    We are now running PHP on GNU Centos Linux!<br />
  </body>
</html>
bash-3.2#
```

PHP and LAMP are very popular web-programming technologies. LAMP installation and configuration is sure to come up on your list of needs as a CentOS Administrator. Easy to use CentOS packages have taken a lot of work from compiling Apache, MySQL, and PHP from the source code.

SET UP PYTHON WITH CENTOS LINUX

Python is a widely used interpreted language that has brought professionalism to the world of coding scripted applications on Linux (and other operating systems). Where Perl was once the industry standard, Python has surpassed Perl in many respects.

Some strengths of Python versus Perl are −

❖ Rapid progression in refinement
❖ Libraries that are standard to the language
❖ Readability of the code is thought out in language definition
❖ Many professional frameworks for everything from GUI support to web-development

Python can do anything Perl can do, and in a lot of cases in a better manner. Though Perl still has its place amongst the toolbox of a Linux admin, learning Python is a great choice as a skill set.

The biggest drawbacks of Python are sometimes related to its strengths. In history, Python was originally designed to teach programming. At times, its core foundations of "easily readable" and "doing things the right way" can cause unnecessary complexities when writing a simple code. Also, its standard libraries have caused problems in transitioning from versions 2.X to 3.X.

Python scripts are actually used at the core of CentOS for functions vital to the functionality of the operating system. Because of this, it is important to isolate our development Python environment from CentOS' core Python environment.

For starters, there are currently two versions of Python: Python 2.X and Python 3.X.

Both stages are still in active production, though version 2.X is quickly closing in on depreciation (and has been for a few years). The reason for the two active versions of Python was basically fixing the shortcomings of version 2.X. This required some core functionality of version 3.X to be redone in ways it could not support some version 2.X scripts.

Basically, the best way to overcome this transition is: Develop for 3.X and keep up with the latest 2.X version for legacy scripts. Currently, CentOS 7.X relies on a semi-current revision of version 2.X.

As of this writing, the most current versions of Python are: 3.4.6 and 2.7.13.

Don't let this confuse or draw any conclusions of Python. Setting up a Python environment is really pretty simple. With Python frameworks and libraries, this task is actually really easy to accomplish.

Before setting up our Python environments, we need a sane environment. To start, let's make sure our CentOS install is fully updated and get some building utilities installed.

Step 1 – Update CentOS.

```
[root@CentOS]# yum -y update
```

Step 2 – Install build utilities.

```
[root@CentOS]# yum -y groupinstall "development tools"
```

Step 3 – Install some needed packages.

```
[root@CentOS]# yum install -y zlib-dev openssl-devel sqlite-devel bip2-devel
```

Now we need to install current Python 2.X and 3.X from source.

- ❖ Download compressed archives
- ❖ Extract files
- ❖ Compile source code

Let's start by creating a build directory for each Python install in /usr/src/

```
[root@CentOS]# mkdir -p /usr/src/pythonSource
```

Now let's download the source tarballs for each –

```
[root@CentOS]# wget https://www.python.org/ftp/python/2.7.13/Python-2.7.13.tar.xz
[root@CentOS]# wget https://www.python.org/ftp/python/3.6.0/Python-3.6.0.tar.xz
```

Now we need to extract each from the archive.

Step 1 – Install xz-libs and extract the tarballs.

```
[root@CentOS]# yum install xz-libs
[root@CentOS python3]# xz -d ./*.xz
[root@CentOS python3]# ls
Python-2.7.13.tar  Python-3.6.0.tar
[root@CentOS python3]#
```

Step 2 – Untar each installer from its tarball.

```
[root@CentOS]# tar -xvf ./Python-2.7.13.tar
[root@CentOS]# tar -xvf ./Python-3.6.0.tar
```

Step 3 – Enter each directory and run the configure script.

```
[root@CentOS]# ./configure --prefix=/usr/local
root@CentOS]# make altinstall
```

Note – Be sure to use altinstall and not install. This will keep CentOS and development versions of Python separated. Otherwise, you may break the functionality of CentOS.

You will now see the compilation process begins. Grab a cup of coffee and take a 15minute break until completion. Since we installed all the needed dependencies for Python, the compilation process should complete without error.

Let's make sure we have the latest 2.X version of Python installed.

```
[root@CentOS Python-2.7.13]# /usr/local/bin/python2.7 -V
Python 2.7.13
[root@CentOS Python-2.7.13]#
```

Note – You will want to prefix the shebang line pointing to our development environment for Python 2.X.

```
[root@CentOS Python-2.7.13]# cat ver.py
#!/usr/local/bin/python2.7
import sys
print(sys.version)
[root@CentOS Python-2.7.13]# ./ver.py
2.7.13 (default, Jan 29 2017, 02:24:08)
[GCC 4.8.5 20150623 (Red Hat 4.8.5-11)]
```

Just like that, we have separate Python installs for versions 2.X and 3.X. From here, we can use each and utilities such as pip and virtualenv to further ease the burden of managing Python environments and package installation.

CONFIGURE RUBY ON CENTOS LINUX

Ruby is a great language for both web development and Linux Administration. Ruby provides many benefits found in all the previous languages discussed: PHP, Python, and Perl.

To install Ruby, it is best to bootstrap through the rbenv which allows the administrators to easily install and manage Ruby Environments.

The other method for installing Ruby is the standard CentOS packages for Ruby. It is advisable to use the rbenv method with all its benefits. CentOS packages will be easier for the non-Ruby savvy.

First, let's get some needed dependencies for rbenv installer.

- ❖ git-core
- ❖ zlib
- ❖ zlib-devel
- ❖ gcc-c++
- ❖ patch
- ❖ readline
- ❖ readline-devel
- ❖ libyaml-devel
- ❖ libffi-devel
- ❖ openssl-devel
- ❖ make
- ❖ bzzip2
- ❖ autoconf
- ❖ automake
- ❖ libtool
- ❖ bison
- ❖ curl
- ❖ sqlite-devel

Most of these packages may already be installed depending on the chosen options and roles when installing CentOS. It is good to install everything we are unsure about as this can lead to less headache when installing packages requiring dependencies.

```
[root@CentOS]# yum -y install git-core zlib zlib-devel gcc-c++ patch readline
readline-devel libyaml-devel libffi-devel openssl-devel make bzip2 autoconf
automake libtool bison curl sqlite-devel
```

Method 1 : rbenv for Dynamic Ruby Development Environments

Now as the user who will be using Ruby −

```
[rdc@CentOS ~]$ git clone https://github.com/rbenv/rbenv.git
[rdc@CentOS ~]$ https://github.com/rbenv/ruby-build.git
```

ruby-build will provide installation features to rbenv –

Note – We need to switch to root or an administration user before running install.sh

```
[rdc@CentOS ruby-build]$ cd ~/ruby-build
[rdc@CentOS ruby-build]# ./install.sh
```

Let's set our shell for rbenv and assure we have installedthe correct options.

```
[rdc@CentOS ~]$ source ~/rbenv/rbenv.d/exec/gem-rehash.bash
[rdc@CentOS ruby-build]$ ~/rbenv/bin/rbenv
rbenv 1.1.0-2-g4f8925a
Usage: rbenv <command> [<args>]
```

Some useful rbenv commands are –

Commands	Action
local	Sets or shows the local application-specific Ruby version
global	Sets or shows the global Ruby version
shell	Sets or shows the shell-specific Ruby version
install	Installs a Ruby version using ruby-build
uninstall	Uninstalls a specific Ruby version
rehash	Rehashes rbenv shims (run this after installing executables)
version	Shows the current Ruby version and its origin
versions	Lists all Ruby versions available to rbenv
which	Displays the full path to an executable
whence	Lists all Ruby versions that contain the given executable

Let's now install Ruby –

```
[rdc@CentOS bin]$ ~/rbenv/bin/rbenv install -v 2.2.1
```

After compilation completes –

```
[rdc@CentOS ~]$ ./ruby -v
ruby 2.2.1p85 (2015-02-26 revision 49769) [x86_64-linux]
[rdc@CentOS ~]$
```

We now have a working Ruby environment with an updated and working version of Ruby 2.X branch.

Method 2 : Install Ruby from CentOS Packages

This is the most simple method. However, it can be limited by the version and gems packaged from CentOS. For serious development work, it is highly recommended to use the rbenv method to install Ruby.

Install Ruby, needed development packages, and some common gems.

```
[root@CentOS rdc]# yum install -y ruby.x86_64 ruby-devel.x86_64 ruby-
libs.x86_64 ruby-gem-json.x86_64 rubygem-rake.noarch
```

Unfortunately, we are left with somewhat outdated version of Ruby.

```
[root@CentOS rdc]# ruby -v
ruby 2.0.0p648 (2015-12-16) [x86_64-linux]
```

```
[root@CentOS rdc]#
```

LINUX ADMIN - SET UP PERL FOR CENTOS LINUX

Perl has been around for a long time. It was originally designed as a reporting language used for parsing text files. With increased popularity, Perl has added a module support or CPAN, sockets, threading, and other features needed in a powerful scripting language.

The biggest advantage of Perl over PHP, Python, or Ruby is: it gets things done with minimal fuss. This philosophy of Perl does not always mean it gets things done the right way. However, for administration tasks on Linux, Perl is considered as the go-to choice for a scripting language.

Some advantages of Perl over Python or Ruby are −

* ❖ Powerful text processing
* ❖ Perl makes writing scripts quick and dirty (usually a Perl script will be several dozen lines shorter than an equivalent in Python or Ruby)
* ❖ Perl can do anything (almost)

Some drawbacks of Perl are −

* ❖ Syntax can be confusing
* ❖ Coding style in Perl can be unique and bog down collaboration
* ❖ Perl is not really Object Oriented
* ❖ Typically, there isn't a lot of thought put into standardization and best-practice when Perl is used.

When deciding whether to use Perl, Python or PHP; the following questions should be asked −

* ❖ Will this application ever need versioning?
* ❖ Will other people ever need to modify the code?
* ❖ Will other people need to use this application?
* ❖ Will this application ever be used on another machine or CPU architecture?

If the answers to all the above are "no", Perl is a good choice and may speed things up in terms of end-results.

With this mentioned, let's configure our CentOS server to use the most recent version of Perl.

Before installing Perl, we need to understand the support for Perl. Officially, Perl is only supported far back as the last two stable versions. So, we want to be sure to keep our development environment isolated from the CentOS version.

The reason for isolation is: if someone releases a tool in Perl to the CentOS community, more than likely it will be modified to work on Perl as shipped with CentOS. However, we also want to have the latest version installed for development purposes. Like Python, CentOS ships Perl focused on the reliability and not cutting edge.

Let's check our current version of Perl on CentOS 7.

```
[root@CentOS]# perl -v
This is perl 5, version 16, subversion 3 (v5.16.3) built for x86_64-linux-thread-multi
```

We are currently running Perl 5.16.3. The most current version as of this writing is: perl-5.24.0

We definitely want to upgrade our version, being able to use up-to-date Perl modules in our code. Fortunately, there is a great tool for maintaining Perl environments and keeping our CentOS version of Perl isolated. It is called perlbrew.

Let's install Perl Brew.

```
[root@CentOS]# curl -L https://install.perlbrew.pl | bash
% Total    % Received % Xferd  Average Speed   Time    Time     Time  Current
                                 Dload  Upload   Total   Spent    Left  Speed
100   170  100   170    0     0    396      0 --:--:-- --:--:-- --:--:--   397
100  1247  100  1247    0     0   1929      0 --:--:-- --:--:-- --:--:--  1929
```

Now that we have Perl Brew installed, let's make an environment for the latest version of Perl.

First, we will need the currently installed version of Perl to bootstrap the perlbrew install. Thus, let's get some needed Perl modules from the CentOS repository.

Note – When available we always want to use CentOS Perl modules versus CPAN with our CentOS Perl installation.

Step 1 – Install CentOS Perl Make::Maker module.

```
[root@CentOS]# yum -y install perl-ExtUtils-MakeMaker.noarch
```

Step 2 – Install the latest version of perl.

```
[root@CentOS build]# source ~/perl5/perlbrew/etc/bashrc
[root@CentOS build]# perlbrew install -n -j4 --threads perl-5.24.1
```

The options we chose for our Perl install are –

- ❖ n – No tests
- ❖ j4 – Execute 4 threads in parallel for the installation routines (we are using a quadcore CPU)
- ❖ threads – Enable threading support for Perl

After our installation has been performed successfully, let's switch to our newest Perl environment.

```
[root@CentOS]# ~/perl5/perlbrew/bin/perlbrew use perl-5.24.1
A sub-shell is launched with perl-5.24.1 as the activated perl. Run 'exit' to finish it.
[root@CentOS]# perl -v
This is perl 5, version 24, subversion 1 (v5.24.1) built for x86_64-linuxthread-multi
(with 1 registered patch, see perl -V for more detail)
Copyright 1987-2017, Larry Wall
Perl may be copied only under the terms of either the Artistic License or the GNU General
Public License, which may be found in the Perl 5 source kit.
Complete documentation for Perl, including FAQ lists, should be found on this system
using "man perl" or "perldoc perl".  If you have access to the Internet, point your
```

Simple perl script printing perl version running within the context of our perlbrew environment −

```
[root@CentOS]# cat ./ver.pl
#!/usr/bin/perl
print $^V . "\n";
[root@CentOS]# perl ./ver.pl
v5.24.1
[root@CentOS]#
```

Once perl is installed, we can load cpan modules with perl brew's cpanm −

```
[root@CentOS]# perl-brew install-cpanm
```

Now let's use the cpanm installer to make the LWP module with our current Perl version of 5.24.1 in perl brew.

Step 1 − Switch to the context of our current Perl version.

```
[root@CentOS ~]# ~/perl5/perlbrew/bin/perlbrew use perl-5.24.1
```

A sub-shell is launched with perl-5.24.1 as the activated perl. Run 'exit' to finish it.

```
[root@CentOS ~]#
```

Step 2 − Install LWP User Agent Perl Module.

```
[root@CentOS ~]# ~/perl5/perlbrew/bin/cpanm -i LWP::UserAgent
```

Step 3 − Now let's test our Perl environment with the new CPAN module.

```
[root@CentOS ~]# cat ./get_header.pl
#!/usr/bin/perl
use LWP;
my $browser = LWP::UserAgent->new();
my $response = $browser->get("http://www.slcc.edu/");
unless(!$response->is_success) {
   print $response->header("Server");
}
[root@CentOS ~]# perl ./get_header.pl
Microsoft-IIS/8.5 [root@CentOS ~]#
```

There you have it! Perl Brew makes isolating perl environments a snap and can be considered as a best practice as things get with Perl.

INSTALL AND CONFIGURE OPEN LDAP

LDAP known as Light Weight Directory Access Protocol is a protocol used for accessing X.500 service containers within an enterprise known from a directory. Those who are familiar with Windows Server Administration can think of LDAP as being very similar in nature to Active Directory. It is even a widely used concept of intertwining Windows workstations into an OpenLDAP CentOS enterprise. On the other spectrum, a CentOS Linux workstation can share resources and participate with the basic functionality in a Windows Domain.

Deploying LDAP on CentOS as a Directory Server Agent, Directory System Agent, or DSA (these acronyms are all one and the same) is similar to older Novell Netware installations using the Directory Tree structure with NDS.

Brief History of LDAP

LDAP was basically created as an efficient way to access X.500 directories with enterprise resources. Both X.500 and LDAP share the same characteristics and are so similar that LDAP clients can access X.500 directories with some helpers. While LDAP also has its own directory server called slapd. The main difference between LDAP and DAP is, the lightweight version is designed to operate over TCP.

While DAP uses the full OSI Model. With the advent of the Internet, TCP/IP and Ethernet prominence in networks of today, it is rare to come across a Directory Services implantation using both DAP and native X.500 enterprise directories outside specific legacy computing models.

The main components used with openldap for CentOS Linux are –

openldap	LDAP support libraries
openldap-server	LDAP server
openldap-clients	LDAP client utilities
openldap-devel	Development libraries for OpenLDAP
compay-openldap	OpenLDAP shared libraries
slapd	Directory server daemon of OpenLDAP
slurpd	Used for LDAP replication across an enterprise domain

Note – When naming your enterprise, it is a best practice to use the .local TLD. Using a .net or .com can cause difficulties when segregating an online and internal domain infrastructure. Imagine the extra work for a company internally using acme.com for both external and internal operations. Hence, it can be wise to have Internet resources called acme.com or acme.net. Then, the local networking enterprise resources is depicted as acme.local. This will entail configuring DNS records, but will pay in simplicity, eloquence and security.

Install Open LDAP on CentOS

Install the openldap, openldap-servers, openldap-clients and migrationstools from YUM.

```
[root@localhost]# yum -y install openldap openldap-servers openldap-clients
migration tools
Loaded plugins: fastestmirror, langpacks
updates
| 3.4 kB  00:00:00
updates/7/x86_64/primary_db
| 2.2 MB  00:00:05
Determining fastest mirrors
(1/2): extras/7/x86_64/primary_db
| 121 kB  00:00:01
(2/2): base/7/x86_64/primary_db
| 5.6 MB  00:00:16
Package openldap-2.4.40-13.el7.x86_64 already installed and latest version
Resolving Dependencies
--> Running transaction check
---> Package openldap-clients.x86_64 0:2.4.40-13.el7 will be installed
---> Package openldap-servers.x86_64 0:2.4.40-13.el7 will be installed
--> Finished Dependency Resolution
base/7/x86_64/group_gz
| 155 kB  00:00:00

Dependencies Resolved

================================================================================
==========
================================================================================
==========
Package              Arch
Version              Repository          Size
================================================================================
==========
================================================================================
==========
Installing:
openldap-clients        x86_64
2.4.40-13.el7        base                188 k
openldap-servers        x86_64
2.4.40-13.el7        base                2.1 M
Transaction Summary
================================================================================
==========
================================================================================
==========
Install  2 Packages
Total download size: 2.3 M
Installed size: 5.3 M
Downloading packages:
Installed:
openldap-clients.x86_64 0:2.4.40-13.el7
openldap-servers.x86_64 0:2.4.40-13.el7
Complete!
[root@localhost]#
```

Now, let's start and enable the slapd service −

```
[root@centos]# systemctl start slapd
[root@centos]# systemctl enable  slapd
```

At this point, let's assure we have our openldap structure in /etc/openldap.

```
root@localhost]# ls /etc/openldap/
certs  check_password.conf  ldap.conf  schema  slapd.d
[root@localhost]#
```

Then make sure our slapd service is running.

```
root@centos]# netstat -antup | grep slapd
tcp     0    0 0.0.0.0:389         0.0.0.0:*           LISTEN    1641/slapd
tcp6    0    0 :::389              :::*                LISTEN    1641/slapd
[root@centos]#
```

Next, let's configure our Open LDAP installation.

Make sure our system ldap user has been created.

```
[root@localhost]# id ldap
uid=55(ldap) gid=55(ldap) groups=55(ldap)
[root@localhost]#
```

Generate our LDAP credentials.

```
[root@localhost]# slappasswd
New password:
Re-enter new password:
{SSHA}20RSyjVv6S6r43DFPeJgASDLlLoSU8g.a10
[root@localhost]#
```

We need to save the output from slappasswd.

Configure Open LDAP

Step 1 – Configure LDAP for domain and add administrative user.

First, we want to set up our openLDAP environment. Following is a template to use with the ldapmodify command.

```
dn: olcDatabase={2}hdb,cn=config
changetype: modify
replace: olcSuffix
olcSuffix: dc=vmnet,dc=local
dn: olcDatabase = {2}hdb,cn=config
changetype: modify
replace: olcRootDN
olcRootDN: cn=ldapadm,dc=vmnet,dc=local
dn: olcDatabase = {2}hdb,cn=config
changetype: modify
replace: olcRootPW
olcRootPW: <output from slap
```

Make changes to: /etc/openldap/slapd.d/cn=config/olcDatabase = {1}monitor.ldif with the ldapmodify command.

```
[root@localhost]# ldapmodify -Y EXTERNAL -H ldapi:/// -f /home/rdc/Documents/db.ldif
SASL/EXTERNAL authentication started
SASL username: gidNumber = 0+uidNumber = 0,cn=peercred,cn=external,cn=auth
SASL SSF: 0
modifying entry "olcDatabase = {2}hdb,cn=config"
modifying entry "olcDatabase = {2}hdb,cn=config"
modifying entry "olcDatabase = {2}hdb,cn=config"
[root@localhost cn=config]#
```

Let's check the modified LDAP configuration.

```
root@linux1 ~]# vi /etc/openldap/slapd.d/cn=config/olcDatabase={2}hdb.ldif
[root@centos]# cat /etc/openldap/slapd.d/cn\=config/olcDatabase\=\{2\}hdb.ldif
 # AUTO-GENERATED FILE - DO NOT EDIT!! Use ldapmodify.
 # CRC32 a163f14c
dn: olcDatabase = {2}hdb
objectClass: olcDatabaseConfig
objectClass: olcHdbConfig
olcDatabase: {2}hdb
olcDbDirectory: /var/lib/ldap
olcDbIndex: objectClass eq,pres
olcDbIndex: ou,cn,mail,surname,givenname eq,pres,sub
structuralObjectClass: olcHdbConfig
entryUUID: 1bd9aa2a-8516-1036-934b-f7eac1189139
creatorsName: cn=config
createTimestamp: 20170212022422Z
olcSuffix: dc=vmnet,dc=local
olcRootDN: cn=ldapadm,dc=vmnet,dc=local
olcRootPW:: e1NTSEF1bUVyb1VzZTRjc2dkYVdGaDY0T0k =
entryCSN: 20170215204423.726622Z#000000#000#000000
modifiersName: gidNumber = 0+uidNumber = 0,cn=peercred,cn=external,cn=auth
modifyTimestamp: 20170215204423Z
[root@centos]#
```

As you can see, our LDAP enterprise modifications were successful.

Next, we want to create an self-signed ssl certificate for OpenLDAP. This will secure the communication between the enterprise server and clients.

Step 2 — Create a self-signed certificate for OpenLDAP.

We will use openssl to create a self-signed ssl certificate. Go to the next chapter, Create LDAP SSL Certificate with openssl for instructions to secure communications with OpenLDAP. Then when ssl certificates are configured, we will have completed our OpenLDAP enterprise configuration.

Step 3 — Configure OpenLDAP to use secure communications with certificate.

Create a certs.ldif file in vim with the following information −

```
dn: cn=config
changetype: modify
replace: olcTLSCertificateFile
olcTLSCertificateFile: /etc/openldap/certs/yourGeneratedCertFile.pem
dn: cn=config
changetype: modify
replace: olcTLSCertificateKeyFile
olcTLSCertificateKeyFile: /etc/openldap/certs/youGeneratedKeyFile.pem
```

Next, again, use the ldapmodify command to merge the changes into the OpenLDAP configuration.

```
[root@centos rdc]# ldapmodify -Y EXTERNAL -H ldapi:/// -f certs.ldif
SASL/EXTERNAL authentication started
SASL username: gidNumber = 0+uidNumber = 0,cn=peercred,cn=external,cn=auth
SASL SSF: 0
modifying entry "cn=config"
[root@centos]#
```

Finally, let's test our OpenLADP configuration.

```
[root@centos]# slaptest -u
config file testing succeeded
[root@centos]#
```

Step 4 – Set up slapd database.

```
cp /usr/share/openldap-servers/DB_CONFIG.example /var/lib/ldap/DB_CONFIG &&
chown ldap:ldap /var/lib/ldap/*
```

Updates the OpenLDAP Schema.

Add the cosine and nis LDAP schemas.

```
ldapadd -Y EXTERNAL -H ldapi:/// -f /etc/openldap/schema/cosine.ldif
ldapadd -Y EXTERNAL -H ldapi:/// -f /etc/openldap/schema/nis.ldif
ldapadd -Y EXTERNAL -H ldapi:/// -f /etc/openldap/schema/inetorgperson.ldif
```

Finally, create the enterprise schema and add it to the current OpenLDAP configuration.

Following is for a domain called vmnet.local with an LDAP Admin called ldapadm.

```
dn: dc=vmnet,dc=local
dc: vmnet
objectClass: top
objectClass: domain
dn: cn=ldapadm ,dc=vmnet,dc=local
objectClass: organizationalRole
cn: ldapadm
description: LDAP Manager
dn: ou = People,dc=vmnet,dc=local
objectClass: organizationalUnit
ou: People
dn: ou = Group,dc=vmnet,dc=local
objectClass: organizationalUnit
ou: Group
```

Finally, import this into the current OpenLDAP schema.

```
[root@centos]# ldapadd -x -W -D "cn=ldapadm,dc=vmnet,dc=local" -f ./base.ldif
 Enter LDAP Password:
adding new entry "dc=vmnet,dc=local"
adding new entry "cn=ldapadm ,dc=vmnet,dc=local"
adding new entry "ou=People,dc=vmnet,dc=local"
adding new entry "ou=Group,dc=vmnet,dc=local"
[root@centos]#
```

Step 5 – Set up an OpenLDAP Enterprise Users.

Open vim or your favorite text editor and copy the following format. This is setup for a user named "entacct" on the "vmnet.local" LDAP domain.

```
dn: uid=entacct,ou=People,dc=vmnet,dc=local
objectClass: top
objectClass: account
objectClass: posixAccount
objectClass: shadowAccount
cn: entacct
uid: entacct
uidNumber: 9999
```

```
gidNumber: 100
homeDirectory: /home/enyacct
loginShell: /bin/bash
gecos: Enterprise User Account 001
userPassword: {crypt}x
shadowLastChange: 17058
shadowMin: 0
shadowMax: 99999
shadowWarning: 7
```

Now import the above files, as saved, into the OpenLdap Schema.

```
[root@centos]# ldapadd -x -W -D "cn=ldapadm,dc=vmnet,dc=local" -f entuser.ldif
Enter LDAP Password:
adding new entry "uid=entacct,ou=People,dc=vmnet,dc=local"
[root@centos]#
```

Before the users can access the LDAP Enterprise, we need to assign a password as follows −

```
ldappasswd -s password123 -W -D "cn=ldapadm,dc=entacct,dc=local" -x "uid=entacct
,ou=People,dc=vmnet,dc=local"
```

-s specifies the password for the user

-x is the username to which password updated is applied

-D is the *distinguished name" to authenticate against LDAP schema.

Finally, before logging into the Enterprise account, let's check our OpenLDAP entry.

```
[root@centos rdc]# ldapsearch -x cn=entacct -b dc=vmnet,dc=local
# extended LDIF
#
# LDAPv3
# base <dc=vmnet,dc=local> with scope subtree
# filter: cn=entacct
# requesting: ALL
#
# entacct, People, vmnet.local
dn: uid=entacct,ou=People,dc=vmnet,dc=local
objectClass: top
objectClass: account
objectClass: posixAccount
objectClass: shadowAccount
cn: entacct
uid: entacct
uidNumber: 9999
gidNumber: 100
homeDirectory: /home/enyacct
loginShell: /bin/bash
gecos: Enterprise User Account 001
userPassword:: e2NyeXB0fXg=
shadowLastChange: 17058
shadowMin: 0
shadowMax: 99999
shadowWarning: 7
```

Converting things like /etc/passwd and /etc/groups to OpenLDAP authentication requires the use of migration tools. These are included in the migrationtools package. Then, installed into /usr/share/migrationtools.

```
[root@centos openldap-servers]# ls -l /usr/share/migrationtools/
total 128
-rwxr-xr-x. 1 root root 2652 Jun  9 2014 migrate_aliases.pl
-rwxr-xr-x. 1 root root 2950 Jun  9 2014 migrate_all_netinfo_offline.sh
-rwxr-xr-x. 1 root root 2946 Jun  9 2014 migrate_all_netinfo_online.sh
-rwxr-xr-x. 1 root root 3011 Jun  9 2014 migrate_all_nis_offline.sh
-rwxr-xr-x. 1 root root 3006 Jun  9 2014 migrate_all_nis_online.sh
-rwxr-xr-x. 1 root root 3164 Jun  9 2014 migrate_all_nisplus_offline.sh
-rwxr-xr-x. 1 root root 3146 Jun  9 2014 migrate_all_nisplus_online.sh
-rwxr-xr-x. 1 root root 5267 Jun  9 2014 migrate_all_offline.sh
-rwxr-xr-x. 1 root root 7468 Jun  9 2014 migrate_all_online.sh
-rwxr-xr-x. 1 root root 3278 Jun  9 2014 migrate_automount.pl
-rwxr-xr-x. 1 root root 2608 Jun  9 2014 migrate_base.pl
```

Step 6 − Finally, we need to allow access to the slapd service so it can service requests.

```
firewall-cmd --permanent --add-service=ldap
firewall-cmd --reload
```

Configure LDAP Client Access

Configuring LDAP client access requires the following packages on the client: openldap, open-ldap clients, and nss_ldap.

Configuring LDAP authentication for client systems is a bit easier.

Step 1 − Install dependent packeges −

```
# yum install -y openldap-clients nss-pam-ldapd
```

Step 2 − Configure LDAP authentication with authconfig.

```
authconfig --enableldap --enableldapauth --ldapserver=10.25.0.1 --
ldapbasedn="dc=vmnet,dc=local" --enablemkhomedir --update
```

Step 3 − Restart nslcd service.

```
systemctl restart nslcd
```

LINUX ADMIN - CREATE SSL CERTIFICATES

TLS and SSL Background

TLS is the new standard for socket layer security, proceeding SSL. TLS offers better encryption standards with other security and protocol wrapper features advancing SSL. Often, the terms TLS and SSL are used interchangeably. However, as a professional CentOS Administrator, it is important to note the differences and history separating each.

SSL goes up to version 3.0. SSL was developed and promoted as an industry standard under Netscape. After Netscape was purchased by AOL (an ISP popular in the 90's otherwise known as America Online) AOL never really promoted the change needed for security improvements to SSL.

At version 3.1, SSL technology moved into the open systems standards and was changed to TLS. Since copyrights on SSL were still owned by AOL a new term was coined: TLS - Transport Layer Security. So it is important to acknowledge that TLS is in fact different from SSL. Especially, as older SSL technologies have known security issues and some are considered obsolete today.

Note — This tutorial will use the term TLS when speaking of technologies 3.1 and higher. Then SSL when commenting specific to SSL technologies 3.0 and lower.

SSL vs TLS Versioning

The following table shows how TLS and SSL versioning would relate to one another. I have heard a few people speak in terms of SSL version 3.2. However, they probably got the terminology from reading a blog. As a professional administrator, we always want to use the standard terminology. Hence, while speaking SSL should be a reference to past technologies. Simple things can make a CentOS job seeker look like a seasoned CS Major.

TLS	SSL
-	3.0
1.0	3.1
1.1	3.2
1.2	3.3

TLS performs two main functions important to the users of the Internet today: One, it verifies who a party is, known as authentication. Two, it offers end-to-end encryption at the transport layer for upper level protocols that lack this native feature (ftp, http, email protocols, and more).

The first, verifies who a party is and is important to security as end-to-end encryption. If a consumer has an encrypted connection to a website that is not authorized to take payment, financial data is still at risk. This is what every phishing site will fail to have: a properly signed TLS certificate verifying website operators are who they claim to be from a trusted CA.

There are only two methods to get around not having a properly signed certificate: trick the user into allowing trust of a web-browser for a self-signed certificate or hope the user is not tech savvy and will not know the importance of a trusted Certificate Authority (or a CA).

In this tutorial, we will be using what is known as a self-signed certificate. This means, without explicitly giving this certificate the status of trusted in every web browser visiting the web-site, an error will be displayed discouraging the users from visiting the site. Then, it will make the user jump though a few actions before accessing a site with a self-signed certificate. Remember for the sake of security this is a good thing.

Install and Configure openssl

openssl is the standard for open-source implementations of TLS. openssl is used on systems such as Linux, BSD distributions, OS X, and even supports Windows.

openssl is important, as it provides transport layer security and abstracts the detailed programming of Authentication and end-to-end encryption for a developer. This is why openssl is used with almost every single open-source application using TLS. It is also installed by default on every modern version of Linux.

By default, openssl should be installed on CentOS from at least version 5 onwards. Just to assure, let's try installing openssl via YUM. Just run install, as YUM is intelligent enough to let us know if a package is already installed. If we are running an older version of CentOS for compatibility reasons, doing a yum -y install will ensure openssl is updated against the semi-recent heart-bleed vulnerability.

When running the installer, it was found there was actually an update to openssl.

```
[root@centos]# yum -y install openssl
Resolving Dependencies
--> Running transaction check
---> Package openssl.x86_64 1:1.0.1e-60.el7 will be updated
---> Package openssl.x86_64 1:1.0.1e-60.el7_3.1 will be an update
--> Processing Dependency: openssl-libs(x86-64) = 1:1.0.1e-60.el7_3.1 for
package: 1:openssl-1.0.1e-60.el7_3.1.x86_64
--> Running transaction check
---> Package openssl-libs.x86_64 1:1.0.1e-60.el7 will be updated
---> Package openssl-libs.x86_64 1:1.0.1e-60.el7_3.1 will be an update
--> Finished Dependency Resolution
Dependencies Resolved
================================================================================
==========
================================================================================
==========
Package                    Arch
Version               Repository          Size
================================================================================
==========
================================================================================
==========
Updating:
openssl                    x86_64
```

Create Self-signed Certificate for OpenLDAP

This is a method to create a self-signed for our previous OpenLDAP installation.

To create an self-signed OpenLDAP Certificate.

```
openssl req -new -x509 -nodes -out /etc/openldap/certs/myldaplocal.pem -keyout
/etc/openldap/certs/myldaplocal.pem -days 365
[root@centos]# openssl req -new -x509 -nodes -out /etc/openldap/certs/vmnet.pem
-keyout /etc/openldap/certs/vmnet.pem -days 365
Generating a 2048 bit RSA private key
............................................+++
............................................+++
writing new private key to '/etc/openldap/certs/vmnet.pem'
-----
You are about to be asked to enter information that will be incorporated
into your certificate request.
What you are about to enter is what is called a Distinguished Name or a DN.
There are quite a few fields but you can leave some blank
For some fields there will be a default value,
If you enter '.', the field will be left blank.
-----
Country Name (2 letter code) [XX]:US
State or Province Name (full name) []:California
Locality Name (eg, city) [Default City]:LA
Organization Name (eg, company) [Default Company Ltd]:vmnet
Organizational Unit Name (eg, section) []:
Common Name (eg, your name or your server's hostname) []:centos
Email Address []:bob@bobber.net
[root@centos]#
```

Now our OpenLDAP certificates should be placed in /etc/openldap/certs/

```
[root@centos]# ls /etc/openldap/certs/*.pem
/etc/openldap/certs/vmnetcert.pem  /etc/openldap/certs/vmnetkey.pem
[root@centos]#
```

As you can see, we have both the certificate and key installed in the /etc/openldap/certs/ directories. Finally, we need to change the permissions to each, since they are currently owned by the root user.

```
[root@centos]# chown -R ldap:ldap /etc/openldap/certs/*.pem
[root@centos]# ls -ld /etc/openldap/certs/*.pem
-rw-r--r--. 1 ldap ldap 1395 Feb 20 10:00 /etc/openldap/certs/vmnetcert.pem
-rw-r--r--. 1 ldap ldap 1704 Feb 20 10:00 /etc/openldap/certs/vmnetkey.pem
[root@centos]#
```

Create Self-signed Certificate for Apache Web Server

In this tutorial, we will assume Apache is already installed. We did install Apache in another tutorial (configuring CentOS Firewall) and will go into advanced installation of Apache for a future tutorial. So, if you have not already installed Apache, please follow along.

Once Apache HTTPd can be installed using the following steps −

Step 1 – Install mod_ssl for Apache httpd server.

First we need to configure Apache with mod_ssl. Using the YUM package manager this is pretty simple –

```
[root@centos]# yum -y install mod_ssl
```

Then reload your Apache daemon to ensure Apache uses the new configuration.

```
[root@centos]# systemctl reload httpd
```

At this point, Apache is configured to support TLS connections on the local host.

Step 2 – Create the self-signed ssl certificate.

First, let's configure our private TLS key directory.

```
[root@centos]# mkdir /etc/ssl/private
[root@centos]# chmod 700 /etc/ssl/private/
```

Note – Be sure only the root has read/write access to this directory. With world read/write access, your private key can be used to decrypt sniffed traffic.

Generating the certificate and key files.

```
[root@centos]# sudo openssl req -x509 -nodes -days 365 -newkey rsa:2048 -keyout
/etc/ssl/private/self-gen-apache.key -out /etc/ssl/certs/self-sign-apache.crt
Generating a 2048 bit RSA private key
..........+++
....+++
-----
Country Name (2 letter code) [XX]:US
State or Province Name (full name) []:xx
Locality Name (eg, city) [Default City]:xxxx
Organization Name (eg, company) [Default Company Ltd]:VMNET
Organizational Unit Name (eg, section) []:
Common Name (eg, your name or your server's hostname) []:centos.vmnet.local
Email Address []:
[root@centos]#
```

Note – You can use public IP Address of the server if you don't have a registered domain name.

Let's take a look at our certificate –

```
[root@centos]# openssl x509 -in self-sign-apache.crt -text -noout
Certificate:
    Data:
        Version: 3 (0x2)
        Serial Number: 17620849408802622302 (0xf489d52d94550b5e)
    Signature Algorithm: sha256WithRSAEncryption
        Issuer: C=US, ST=UT, L=xxxx, O=VMNET, CN=centos.vmnet.local
        Validity
            Not Before: Feb 24 07:07:55 2017 GMT
            Not After : Feb 24 07:07:55 2018 GMT
        Subject: C=US, ST=UT, L=xxxx, O=VMNET, CN=centos.vmnet.local
        Subject Public Key Info:
            Public Key Algorithm: rsaEncryption
                Public-Key: (2048 bit)
                Modulus:
                    00:c1:74:3e:fc:03:ca:06:95:8d:3a:0b:7e:1a:56:
                    f3:8d:de:c4:7e:ee:f9:fa:79:82:bf:db:a9:6d:2a:
                    57:e5:4c:31:83:cf:92:c4:e7:16:57:59:02:9e:38:
```

```
47:00:cd:b8:31:b8:34:55:1c:a3:5d:cd:b4:8c:b0:
66:0c:0c:81:8b:7e:65:26:50:9d:b7:ab:78:95:a5:
31:5e:87:81:cd:43:fc:4d:00:47:5e:06:d0:cb:71:
9b:2a:ab:f0:90:ce:81:45:0d:ae:a8:84:80:c5:0e:
79:8a:c1:9b:f4:38:5d:9e:94:4e:3a:3f:bd:cc:89:
e5:96:4a:44:f5:3d:13:20:3d:6a:c6:4d:91:be:aa:
ef:2e:d5:81:ea:82:c6:09:4f:40:74:c1:b1:37:6c:
ff:50:08:dc:c8:f0:67:75:12:ab:cd:8d:3e:7b:59:
e0:83:64:5d:0c:ab:93:e2:1c:78:f0:f4:80:9e:42:
7d:49:57:71:a2:96:c6:b8:44:16:93:6c:62:87:0f:
5c:fe:df:29:89:03:6e:e5:6d:db:0a:65:b2:5e:1d:
c8:07:3d:8a:f0:6c:7f:f3:b9:32:b4:97:f6:71:81:
6b:97:e3:08:bd:d6:f8:19:40:f1:15:7e:f2:fd:a5:
12:24:08:39:fa:b6:cc:69:4e:53:1d:7e:9a:be:4b:
```

Here is an explanation for each option we used with the openssl command –

Command	Action
req -X509	Use X.509 CSR management PKI standard for key management.
-nodes	Do not secure our certificate with a passphrase. Apache must be able to use the certificate without interruption of a passphrase.
-days 2555	Tells the validity of the certificate to 7 years or 2555 days. Time period can be adjusted as needed.
-newkey rsa:2048	Specified to generate both key and certificate using RSA at 2048 bits in length.

Next, we want to create a Diffie-Hellman group for negotiating PFS with clients.

```
[centos#] openssl dhparam -out /etc/ssl/certs/dhparam.pem 2048
```

This will take from 5 to 15 minutes.

Perfect Forward Secrecy – Used to secure session data in case the private key has been compromised. This will generate a key used between the client and the server that is unique for each session.

Now, add the Perfect Forward Secrecy configuration to our certificate.

```
[root@centos]# cat /etc/ssl/certs/dhparam.pem | tee -a /etc/ssl/certs/self-sign-apache.crt
```

Configure Apache to Use Key and Certificate Files

We will be making changes to /etc/httpd/conf.d/ssl.conf –

We will make the following changes to ssl.conf. However, before we do that we should back the original file up. When making changes to a production server in an advanced text editor like vi or emcas, it is a best practice to always backup configuration files before making edits.

```
[root@centos]# cp /etc/httpd/conf.d/ssl.conf ~/
```

Now let's continue our edits after copying a known-working copy of ssl.conf to the root of our home folder.

- ❖ Locate
- ❖ Edit both DocumentRoot and ServerName as follows.

```
\\# General setup for the virtual host, inherited from global configuration
DocumentRoot "/var/www/html"
ServerName centos.vmnet.local:443
```

DocumentRoot this is the path to your default apache directory. In this folder should be a default page that will display a HTTP request asking for the default page of your web server or site.

ServerName is the server name that can be either an ip address or the host name of the server. For TLS, it is a best practice to create a certificate with a host name. From our OpenLdap tutorial, we created a hostname of centos on the local enterprise domain: vmnet.local

Now we want to comment the following lines out.

SSLProtocol

```
#   SSL Protocol support:
# List the enable protocol levels with which clients will be able to
# connect.  Disable SSLv2 access by default:
~~~~> #SSLProtocol all -SSLv2

#   SSL Cipher Suite:
# List the ciphers that the client is permitted to negotiate.
# See the mod_ssl documentation for a complete list.
~~~~> #SSLCipherSuite HIGH:MEDIUM:!aNULL:!MD5:!SEED:!IDEA
```

Then let Apache know where to find our certificate and private/public key pair.

Specify path to our self-signed certificate file

```
#   Server Certificate:
# Point SSLCertificateFile at a PEM encoded certificate.  If
# the certificate is encrypted, then you will be prompted for a
# pass phrase.  Note that a kill -HUP will prompt again.  A new
# certificate can be generated using the genkey(1) command.
~~~~> SSLCertificateFile /etc/ssl/certs/self-sign-apache.crt
specify path to our private key file
#   Server Private Key:
# If the key is not combined with the certificate, use this
# directive to point at the key file.  Keep in mind that if
# you've both a RSA and a DSA private key you can configure
# both in parallel (to also allow the use of DSA ciphers, etc.)
~~~~> SSLCertificateKeyFile /etc/ssl/private/self-gen-apache.key
```

Finally, we need to allow inbound connections to https over port 443.

INSTALL APACHE WEB SERVER CENTOS 7

In this chapter, we will learn a little about the background of how Apache HTTP Server came into existence and then install the most current stable version on CentOS Linux 7.

Brief History on Apache WebServer

Apache is a web server that has been around for a long time. In fact, almost as long as the existence of http itself!

Apache started out as a rather small project at the National Center for Supercomputing Applications also known as NCSA. In the mid-90's "httpd", as it was called, was by far the most popular web-server platform on the Internet, having about 90% or more of the market share.

At this time, it was a simple project. Skilled I.T. staff known as webmaster were responsible for: maintaining web server platforms and web server software as well as both front-end and back-end site development. At the core of httpd was its ability to use custom modules known as plugins or extensions. A webmaster was also skilled enough to write patches to core server software.

Sometime in the late-mid-90's, the senior developer and project manager for httpd left NCSA to do other things. This left the most popular web-daemon in a state of stagnation.

Since the use of httpd was so widespread a group of seasoned httpd webmasters called for a summit reqarding the future of httpd. It was decided to coordinate and apply the best extensions and patches into a current stable release. Then, the current grand-daddy of http servers was born and christened Apache HTTP Server.

Little Known Historical Fact – Apache was not named after a Native American Tribe of warriors. It was in fact coined and named with a twist: being made from many fixes (or patches) from many talented Computer Scientists: a patchy or Apache.

Install Current Stable Version on CentOS Linux 7

Step 1 – Install httpd via yum.

```
yum -y install httpd
```

At this point Apache HTTP Server will install via yum.

Step 2 – Edit httpd.conf file specific to your httpd needs.

With a default Apache install, the configuration file for Apache is named httpd.conf and is located in /etc/httpd/. So, let's open it in vim.

The first few lines of httpd.conf opened in vim –

```
#
# This is the main Apache HTTP server configuration file.  It contains the
# configuration directives that give the server its instructions.
# See <URL:http://httpd.apache.org/docs/2.4/> for detailed information.
# In particular, see
# <URL:http://httpd.apache.org/docs/2.4/mod/directives.html>
# for a discussion of each configuration directive.
```

We will make the following changes to allow our CentOS install to serve http requests from http port 80.

Listening host and port

```
# Listen: Allows you to bind Apache to specific IP addresses and/or
# ports, instead of the default. See also the <VirtualHost>
# directive.
#
# Change this to Listen on specific IP addresses as shown below to
# prevent Apache from glomming onto all bound IP addresses.
#
#Listen 12.34.56.78:80
Listen 80
```

From here, we change Apache to listen on a certain port or IP Address. For example, if we want to run httpd services on an alternative port such as 8080. Or if we have our web-server configured with multiple interfaces with separate IP addresses.

Listen

Keeps Apache from attaching to every listening daemon onto every IP Address. This is useful to stop specifying only IPv6 or IPv4 traffic. Or even binding to all network interfaces on a multi-homed host.

```
#
# Listen: Allows you to bind Apache to specific IP addresses and/or
# ports, instead of the default. See also the <VirtualHost>
# directive.
#
# Change this to Listen on specific IP addresses as shown below to
# prevent Apache from glomming onto all bound IP addresses.
#
Listen 10.0.0.25:80
#Listen 80
```

DocumentRoot

The "document root" is the default directory where Apache will look for an index file to serve for requests upon visiting your sever: http://www.yoursite.com/ will retrieve and serve the index file from your document root.

```
#
# DocumentRoot: The directory out of which you will serve your
# documents. By default, all requests are taken from this directory, but
# symbolic links and aliases may be used to point to other locations.
#
```

DocumentRoot "/var/www/html"

Step 3 — Start and Enable the httpd Service.

```
[root@centos rdc]# systemctl start httpd && systemctl reload httpd
[root@centos rdc]#
```

Step 4 — Configure firewall to allow access to port 80 requests.

```
[root@centos]# firewall-cmd --add-service=http --permanent
```

As touched upon briefly when configuring CentOS for use with Maria DB, there is no native MySQL package in the CentOS 7 yum repository. To account for this, we will need to add a MySQL hosted repository.

MariaDB vs MySQL On CentOS Linux

One thing to note is MySQL will require a different set of base dependencies from MariaDB. Also using MySQL will break the concept and philosophy of CentOS: production packages designed for maximum reliability.

So when deciding whether to use Maria or MySQL one should weigh two options: Will my current DB Schema work with Maria? What advantage does installing MySQL over Maria give me?

Maria components are 100% transparent to MySQL structure, with some added efficiency with better licensing. Unless a compelling reason comes along, it is advised to configure CentOS to use MariaDB.

The biggest reasons for favoring Maria on CentOS are −

❖ Most people will be using MariaDB. When experiencing issues you will get more assistance with Maria.
❖ CentOS is designed to run with Maria. Hence, Maria will offer better stability.
❖ Maria is officially supported for CentOS.

Download and Add the MySQL Repository

We will want to download and install the MySQL repository from −

http://repo.mysql.com/mysql-community-release-el7-5.noarch.rpm

Step 1 − Download the Repository.

The repository comes conveniently packaged in an rpm package for easy installation. It can be downloaded with wget −

```
[root@centos]# wget http://repo.mysql.com/mysql-community-release-el75.noarch.rpm
--2017-02-26 03:18:36--  http://repo.mysql.com/mysql-community-release-el75.noarch.rpm
Resolving repo.mysql.com (repo.mysql.com)... 104.86.98.130
```

Step 2 − Install MySQL From YUM.

We can now use the yum package manager to install MySQL −

```
[root@centos]# yum -y install mysql-server
```

Step 3 − Start and Enable the MySQL Daemon Service.

```
[root@centos]# systemctl start mysql
[root@centos]# systemctl enable  mysql
```

Step 4 – Make sure our MySQL service is up and running.

```
[root@centos]# netstat -antup | grep 3306
tcp6    0    0 :::3306    :::*    LISTEN    6572/mysqld
[root@centos]#
```

Note – We will not allow any firewall rules through. It's common to have MySQL configured to use Unix Domain Sockets. This assures only the web-server of the LAMP stack, locally, can access the MySQL database, taking out a complete dimension in the attack vector at the database software.

SET UP POSTFIX MTA AND IMAP/POP3

In order to send an email from our CentOS 7 server, we will need the setup to configure a modern Mail Transfer Agent (MTA). Mail Transfer Agent is the daemon responsible for sending outbound mail for system users or corporate Internet Domains via SMTP.

It is worth noting, this tutorial only teaches the process of setting up the daemon for local use. We do not go into detail about advanced configuration for setting up an MTA for business operations. This is a combination of many skills including but not limited to: DNS, getting a static routable IP address that is not blacklisted, and configuring advanced security and service settings. In short, this tutorial is meant to familiarize you with the basic configuration. Do not use this tutorial for MTA configuration of an Internet facing host.

With its combined focus on both security and the ease of administration, we have chosen Postfix as the MTA for this tutorial. The default MTA installed in the older versions of CentOS is Sendmail. Sendmail is a great MTA. However, of the author's humble opinion, Postfix hits a sweet spot when addressing the following notes for an MTA. With the most current version of CentOS, Postfix has superseded Sendmail as the default MTA.

Postfix is a widely used and well documented MTA. It is actively maintained and developed. It requires minimal configuration in mind (this is just email) and is efficient with system resources (again, this is just email).

Step 1 – Install Postfix from YUM Package Manager.

```
[root@centos]# yum -y install postfix
```

Step 2 – Configure Postfix config file.

The Postfix configuration file is located in: /etc/postfix/main.cf

In a simple Postfix configuration, the following must be configured for a specific host: host name, domain, origin, inet_interfaces, and destination.

Configure the hostname – The hostname is a fully qualified domain name of the Postfix host. In OpenLDAP chapter, we named the CentOS box: centos on the domain vmnet.local. Let's stick with that for this chapter.

```
# The myhostname parameter specifies the internet hostname of this
# mail system. The default is to use the fully-qualified domain name
# from gethostname(). $myhostname is used as a default value for many
# other configuration parameters.
#
myhostname = centos.vmnet.local
```

Configure the domain – As stated above, the domain we will be using in this tutorial is vmnet.local

```
# The mydomain parameter specifies the local internet domain name.
# The default is to use $myhostname minus the first component.
```

```
# $mydomain is used as a default value for many other configuration
# parameters.
#
mydomain = vmnet.local
```

Configure the origin – For a single server and domain set up, we just need to uncomment the following sections and leave the default Postfix variables.

```
# SENDING MAIL
#
# The myorigin parameter specifies the domain that locally-posted
# mail appears to come from. The default is to append $myhostname,
# which is fine for small sites. If you run a domain with multiple
# machines, you should (1) change this to $mydomain and (2) set up
# a domain-wide alias database that aliases each user to
# user@that.users.mailhost.
#
# For the sake of consistency between sender and recipient addresses,
# myorigin also specifies the default domain name that is appended
# to recipient addresses that have no @domain part.
#
myorigin = $myhostname
myorigin = $mydomain
```

Configure the network interfaces – We will leave Postfix listening on our single network interface and all protocols and IP Addresses associated with that interface. This is done by simply leaving the default settings enabled for Postfix.

```
# The inet_interfaces parameter specifies the network interface
# addresses that this mail system receives mail on. By default,
# the software claims all active interfaces on the machine. The
# parameter also controls delivery of mail to user@[ip.address].
#
# See also the proxy_interfaces parameter, for network addresses that
# are forwarded to us via a proxy or network address translator.
#
# Note: you need to stop/start Postfix when this parameter changes.
#
#inet_interfaces = all
#inet_interfaces = $myhostname
#inet_interfaces = $myhostname, localhost
#inet_interfaces = localhost
# Enable IPv4, and IPv6 if supported
inet_protocols = all
```

Step 3 – Configure SASL Support for Postfix.

Without SASL Authentication support, Postfix will only allow sending email from local users. Or it will give a relaying denied error when the users send email away from the local domain.

Note – SASL or Simple Application Security Layer Framework is a framework designed for authentication supporting different techniques amongst different Application Layer protocols. Instead of leaving authentication mechanisms up to the application layer protocol, SASL developers (and consumers) leverage current authentication protocols for higher level protocols that may not have the convenience or more secure authentication (when speaking of access to secured services) built in.

Install the "cyrus-sasl* package

```
[root@centos]# yum -y install cyrus-sasl
Loaded plugins: fastestmirror, langpacks
Loading mirror speeds from cached hostfile
 * base: repos.forethought.net
 * extras: repos.dfw.quadranet.com
 * updates: mirrors.tummy.com
Package cyrus-sasl-2.1.26-20.el7_2.x86_64 already installed and latest version
Nothing to do
```

Configure /etc/postfix/main.cf for SASL Auth

```
smtpd_sasl_auth_enable = yes
smtpd_recipient_restrictions =
permit_mynetworks,permit_sasl_authenticated,reject_unauth_destination
smtpd_sasl_security_options = noanonymous
smtpd_sasl_type = dovecot
smtpd_sasl_path = private/auth
```

My SASL Options in main.conf

```
##Configure SASL Options Entries:
smtpd_sasl_auth_enable = yes
smptd_recipient_restrictions =
permit_mynetworks,permit_sasl_authenticated,reject_unauth_destination
smtp_sasl_type = dovecot
smtp_sasl_path = private/auth/etc
```

Step 4 – Configure FirewallD to allow incoming SMTP Services.

```
[root@centos]# firewall-cmd --permanent --add-service=smtp
success
[root@centos]# firewall-cmd --reload
success
[root@centos]#
```

Now let's check to make sure our CentOS host is allowing and responding to the requests on port 25 (SMTP).

```
Nmap scan report for 172.16.223.132
Host is up (0.00035s latency).
Not shown: 993 filtered ports
PORT    STATE  SERVICE
  20/tcp  closed ftp-data
  21/tcp  open   ftp
  22/tcp  open   ssh
  25/tcp  open   smtp
  80/tcp  open   http
  389/tcp open   ldap
  443/tcp open   https
MAC Address: 00:0C:29:BE:DF:5F (VMware)
```

As you can see, SMTP is listening and the daemon is responding to the requests from our internal LAN.

Install Dovecot IMAP and POP3 Server

Dovecot is a secure IMAP and POP3 Server deigned to handle incoming mail needs of a smaller to larger organization. Due to its prolific use with CentOS, we will be using Dovecot as an example of installing and configuring an incoming mail-server for CentOS and MTA SASL Provider.

As noted previously, we will not be configuring MX records for DNS or creating secure rules allowing our services to handle mail for a domain. Hence, just setting these services up on an Internet facing host may leave leverage room for security holes w/o SPF Records.

Step 1 − Install Dovecot.

```
[root@centos]# yum -y install dovecot
```

Step 2 − Configure dovecot.

The main configuration file for dovecot is located at: /etc/dovecot.conf. We will first back up the main configuration file. It is a good practice to always backup configuration files before making edits. This way id (for example) line breaks get destroyed by a text editor, and years of changes are lost. Reverting is easy as copying the current backup into production.

Enable protocols and daemon service for dovecot

```
# Protocols we want to be serving.
protocols = imap imaps pop3 pop3s
```

Now, we need to enable the dovecot daemon to listen on startup −

```
[root@localhost]# systemctl start dovecot
[root@localhost]# systemctl enable dovecot
```

Let's make sure Dovecot is listening locally on the specified ports for: imap, pop3, imap secured, and pop3 secured.

```
[root@localhost]# netstat -antup | grep dovecot
tcp    0    0 0.0.0.0:110    0.0.0.0:*    LISTEN    4368/dovecot
tcp    0    0 0.0.0.0:143    0.0.0.0:*    LISTEN    4368/dovecot
tcp    0    0 0.0.0.0:993    0.0.0.0:*    LISTEN    4368/dovecot
tcp    0    0 0.0.0.0:995    0.0.0.0:*    LISTEN    4368/dovecot
tcp6   0    0 :::110    :::*    LISTEN    4368/dovecot
tcp6   0    0 :::143    :::*    LISTEN    4368/dovecot
tcp6   0    0 :::993    :::*    LISTEN    4368/dovecot
tcp6   0    0 :::995    :::*    LISTEN    4368/dovecot
[root@localhost]#
```

As seen, dovecot is listening on the specified ports for IPv4 and IPv4.

POP3	110
POP3s	995
IMAP	143
IMAPs	993

Now, we need to make some firewall rules.

```
[root@localhost]# firewall-cmd --permanent --add-port=110/tcp
success
```

```
[root@localhost]# firewall-cmd --permanent --add-port=143/tcp
success
```

```
[root@localhost]# firewall-cmd --permanent --add-port=995/tcp
success

[root@localhost]# firewall-cmd --permanent --add-port=993/tcp
success

[root@localhost]# firewall-cmd --reload
success

[root@localhost]#
```

Our incoming mail sever is accepting requests for POP3, POP3s, IMAP, and IMAPs to hosts on the LAN.

```
Port Scanning host: 192.168.1.143
  Open TCP Port:  21     ftp
  Open TCP Port:  22     ssh
  Open TCP Port:  25     smtp
  Open TCP Port:  80     http
  Open TCP Port:  110    pop3
  Open TCP Port:  143    imap
  Open TCP Port:  443    https
  Open TCP Port:  993    imaps
  Open TCP Port:  995    pop3s
```

LINUX ADMIN - INSTALL ANONYMOUS FTP

Before delving into installing FTP on CentOS, we need to learn a little about its use and security. FTP is a really efficient and well-refined protocol for transferring files between the computer systems. FTP has been used and refined for a few decades now. For transferring files efficiently over a network with latency or for sheer speed, FTP is a great choice. More so than either SAMBA or SMB.

However, FTP does possess some security issues. Actually, some serious security issues. FTP uses a really weak plain-text authentication method. It is for this reason authenticated sessions should rely on sFTP or FTPS, where TLS is used for end-to-end encryption of the login and transfer sessions.

With the above caveats, plain old FTP still has its use in the business environment today. The main use is, anonymous FTP file repositories. This is a situation where no authentication is warranted to download or upload files. Some examples of anonymous FTP use are −

- ❖ Large software companies still use anonymous ftp repositories allowing Internet users to download shareware and patches.
- ❖ Allowing internet users to upload and download public documents.
- ❖ Some applications will automatically send encrypted, archived logs for or configuration files to a repository via FTP.

Hence, as a CentOS Administrator, being able to install and configure FTP is still a designed skill.

We will be using an FTP daemon called vsFTP, or Very Secure FTP Daemon. vsFTP has been used in development for a while. It has a reputation for being secure, easy to install and configure, and is reliable.

Step 1 − Install vsFTPd with the YUM Package Manager.

```
[root@centos]# yum -y install vsftpd.x86_64
```

Step 2 − Configure vsFTP to Start on Boot with systemctl.

```
[root@centos]# systemctl start vsftpd
[root@centos]# systemctl enable vsftpd
Created symlink from /etc/systemd/system/multi-
user.target.wants/vsftpd.service to /usr/lib/systemd/system/vsftpd.service.
```

Step 3 − Configure FirewallD to allow FTP control and transfer sessions.

```
[root@centos]# firewall-cmd --add-service=ftp --permanent
success
[root@centos]#
```

Assure our FTP daemon is running.

```
[root@centos]# netstat -antup | grep vsftp
tcp6    0    0 :::21    :::*    LISTEN    13906/vsftpd
[root@centos]#
```

Step 4 – Configure vsFTPD For Anonymous Access.

Create a root FTP directory

```
[root@centos]# mkdir /ftp
```

Change owner and group of FTP root to ftp

```
[root@centos]# chown ftp:ftp /ftp
Set minimal permissions for FTP root:
[root@centos]# chmod -R 666 /ftp/
[root@centos]# ls -ld /ftp/
drw-rw-rw-. 2 ftp ftp 6 Feb 27 02:01 /ftp/
[root@centos]#
```

In this case, we gave users read/write access to the entire root FTP tree.

Configure /etc/vsftpd/vsftpd.conf"

```
[root@centos]# vim /etc/vsftpd/vsftpd.conf
# Example config file /etc/vsftpd/vsftpd.conf
#
# The default compiled in settings are fairly paranoid. This sample file
# loosens things up a bit, to make the ftp daemon more usable.
# Please see vsftpd.conf.5 for all compiled in defaults.
#
# READ THIS: This example file is NOT an exhaustive list of vsftpd options.
# Please read the vsftpd.conf.5 manual page to get a full idea of vsftpd's
# capabilities.
```

We will want to change the following directives in the vsftp.conf file.

❖ Enable Anonymous uploading by uncommenting
anon_mkdir_write_enable=YES
❖ chown uploaded files to owned by the system ftp user
chown_uploads = YES
chown_username = ftp
❖ Change system user used by vsftp to the ftp user: nopriv_user = ftp
❖ Set the custom banner for the user to read before signing in.
ftpd_banner = Welcome to our Anonymous FTP Repo. All connections
are monitored and logged.
❖ Let's set IPv4 connections only –
listen = YES
listen_ipv6 = NO

Now, we need to restart or HUP the vsftp service to apply our changes.

```
[root@centos]# systemctl restart vsftpd
```

Let's connect to our FTP host and make sure our FTP daemon is responding.

```
[root@centos rdc]# ftp 10.0.4.34
Connected to localhost (10.0.4.34).
220 Welcome to our Anonymous FTP Repo. All connections are monitored and logged.
Name (localhost:root): anonymous
331 Please specify the password.
Password:
```

```
'230 Login successful.
Remote system type is UNIX.
Using binary mode to transfer files.
ftp>
```

LINUX ADMIN - REMOTE MANAGEMENT

When talking about remote management in CentOS as an Administrator, we will explore two methods —

- ❖ Console Management
- ❖ GUI Management

Remote Console Management

Remote Console Management means performing administration tasks from the command line via a service such as ssh. To use CentOS Linux effectively, as an Administrator, you will need to be proficient with the command line. Linux at its heart was designed to be used from the console. Even today, some system administrators prefer the power of the command and save money on the hardware by running bare-bones Linux boxes with no physical terminal and no GUI installed.

Remote GUI Management

Remote GUI Management is usually accomplished in two ways: either a remote X-Session or a GUI application layer protocol like VNC. Each has its strengths and drawbacks. However, for the most part, VNC is the best choice for Administration. It allows graphical control from other operating systems such as Windows or OS X that do not natively support the X Windows protocol.

Using remote X Sessions is native to both X-Window's Window-Managers and DesktopManagers running on X. However, the entire X Session architecture is mostly used with Linux. Not every System Administrator will have a Linux Laptop on hand to establish a remote X Session. Therefore, it is most common to use an adapted version of VNC Server.

The biggest drawbacks to VNC are: VNC does not natively support a multi-user environment such as remote X-Sessions. Hence, for GUI access to end-users remote XSessions would be the best choice. However, we are mainly concerned with administering a CentOS server remotely.

We will discuss configuring VNC for multiple administrators versus a few hundred endusers with remote X-Sessions.

Laying the Foundation for Security with SSH for Remote Console Access

ssh or Secure Shell is now the standard for remotely administering any Linux server. SSH unlike telnet uses TLS for authenticity and end-to-end encryption of communications. When properly configured an administrator can be pretty sure both their password and the server are trusted remotely.

Before configuring SSH, lets talk a little about the basic security and least common access. When SSH is running on its default port of 22; sooner rather than later, you are going to get brute force dictionary attacks against common user names and passwords. This just comes with the territory. No matter how many hosts you add to your deny files, they will just come in from different IP addresses daily.

With a few common rules, you can simply take some pro-active steps and let the bad guys waste their time. Following are a few rules of security to follow using SSH for remote administration on a production server −

- ❖ Never use a common username or password. Usernames on the system should not be system default, or associated with the company email address like: systemadmin@yourcompany.com
- ❖ Root access or administration access should not be allowed via SSH. Use a unique username and su to root or an administration account once authenticated through SSH.
- ❖ Password policy is a must: Complex SSH user passwords like: "This&IS&a&GUD&P@ssW0rd&24&me". Change passwords every few months to eliminate susceptibility to incremental brute force attacks.
- ❖ Disable abandoned or accounts that are unused for extended periods. If a hiring manager has a voicemail stating they will not be doing interviews for a month; that can lead to tech-savvy individuals with a lot time on their hands, for example.
- ❖ Watch your logs daily. As a System Administrator, dedicate at least 30-40 minutes every morning reviewing system and security logs. If asked, let everyone know you don't have the time to not be proactive. This practice will help isolate warning signs before a problem presents itself to end-users and company profits.

Note On Linux Security − Anyone interested in Linux Administration should actively pursue current Cyber-Security news and technology. While we mostly hear about other operating systems being compromised, an insecure Linux box is a sought-after treasure for cybercriminals. With the power of Linux on a high-speed internet connection, a skilled cybercriminal can use Linux to leverage attacks on other operating systems.

Install and Configure SSH for Remote Access

Step 1 − Install SSH Server and all dependent packages.

```
[root@localhost]# yum -y install openssh-server
'Loaded plugins: fastestmirror, langpacks
Loading mirror speeds from cached hostfile
* base: repos.centos.net
* extras: repos.dfw.centos.com
* updates: centos.centos.com
Resolving Dependencies
 --> Running transaction check
 ---> Package openssh-server.x86_64 0:6.6.1p1-33.el7_3 will be installed
 --> Finished Dependency Resolution
Dependencies Resolved
```

Step 2 – Make a secure regular use to add for shell access.

```
[root@localhost ~]# useradd choozer
[root@localhost ~]# usermod -c "Remote Access" -d /home/choozer -g users -G
wheel -a choozer
```

Note – We added the new user to the wheel group enabling ability to su into root once SSH access has been authenticated. We also used a username that cannot be found in common word lists. This way, our account will not get locked out when SSH is attacked.

The file holding configuration settings for sshd server is /etc/ssh/sshd_config.

The portions we want to edit initially are –

```
LoginGraceTime 60m
PermitRootLogin no
```

Step 3 – Reload the SSH daemon sshd.

```
[root@localhost]# systemctl reload sshd
```

It is good to set the logout grace period to 60 minutes. Some complex administration tasks can exceed the default of 2 minutes. There is really nothing more frustrating than having SSH session timeout when configuring or researching changes.

Step 4 – Let's try to login using the root credentials.

```
bash-3.2# ssh centos.vmnet.local
root@centos.vmnet.local's password:
Permission denied (publickey,gssapi-keyex,gssapi-with-mic,password).
```

Step 5 – We can no longer login remotely via ssh with root credentials. So let's login to our unprivileged user account and su into the root account.

```
bash-3.2# ssh chooser@centos.vmnet.local
choozer@centos.vmnet.local's password:
[choozer@localhost ~]$ su root
Password:
[root@localhost choozer]#
```

Step 6 – Finally, let's make sure the SSHD service loads on boot and firewalld allows outside SSH connections.

```
[root@localhost]# systemctl enable sshd
[root@localhost]# firewall-cmd --permanent --add-service=ssh
success
[root@localhost]# firewall-cmd --reload
success

[root@localhost]#
```

SSH is now set up and ready for remote administration. Depending on your enterprise border, the packet filtering border device may need to be configured to allow SSH remote administration outside the corporate LAN.

Configure VNC for Remote CentOS Administration

There are a few ways to enable remote CentOS administration via VNC on CentOS 6 - 7. The easiest, but most limiting way is simply using a package called vino. Vino is a Virtual Network Desktop Connection application for Linux designed around the Gnome Desktop platform. Hence, it is assumed the installation was completed with Gnome Desktop. If the Gnome Desktop has not been installed, please do so before continuing. Vino will be installed with a Gnome GUI install by default.

To configure screen sharing with Vino under Gnome, we want to go into the CentOS System Preferences for screen sharing.

Applications->System Tools->Settings->Sharing

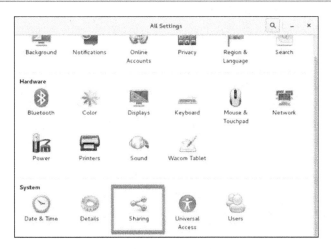

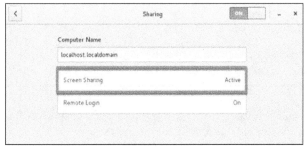

Notes to configuring VNC Desktop Sharing –

- ❖ Disable New Connections must ask for access – This option will require physical access to ok every connection. This option will prevent remote administration unless someone is at the physical desktop.
- ❖ Enable Require a password – This is separate from the user password. It will control the access to the virtual desktop and still require the user password to access a locked desktop (this is good for security).
- ❖ Forward UP&P Ports: If available leave disabled – Forwarding UP&P ports will send Universal Plug and Play requests for a layer 3 device to allow VNC connections to the host automatically. We do not want this.

Make sure vino is listening on the VNC Port 5900.

```
[root@localhost]# netstat -antup | grep vino
tcp    0    0 0.0.0.0:5900    0.0.0.0:*    LISTEN    4873/vino-server
tcp6   0    0 :::5900         :::*         LISTEN    4873/vino-server

[root@localhost]#
```

Let's now configure our Firewall to allow incoming VNC connections.

```
[root@localhost]# firewall-cmd --permanent --add-port=5900/tcp
success
[root@localhost]# firewall-cmd --reload
success
[root@localhost rdc]#
```

Finally, as you can see we are able to connect our CentOS Box and administer it with a VNC client on either Windows or OS X.

It is just as important to obey the same rules for VNC as we set forth for SSH. Just like SSH, VNC is continually scanned across IP ranges and tested for weak passwords. It is also worth a note that leaving the default CentOS login enabled with a console timeout does help with remote VNC security. As an attacker will need the VNC and user password, make sure your screen sharing password is different and just as hard to guess as the user password.

After entering the the VNC screen sharing password, we must also enter the user password to access a locked desktop.

Security Note – By default, VNC is not an encrypted protocol. Hence, the VNC connection should be tunneled through SSH for encryption.

Set Up SSH Tunnel Through VNC

Setting up an SSH Tunnel will provide a layer of SSH encryption to tunnel the VNC connection through. Another great feature is it uses SSH compression to add another layer of compression to the VNC GUI screen updates. More secure and faster is always a good thing when dealing with the administration of CentOS servers!

So from your client that will be initiating the VNC connection, let's set up a remote SSH tunnel. In this demonstration, we are using OS X. First we need to sudo -s to root.

```
bash-3.2# sudo -s
password:
```

Enter the user password and we should now have root shell with a # prompt –

```
bash-3.2#
```

Now, let's create our SSH Tunnel.

```
ssh -f rdc@192.168.1.143 -L 2200:192.168.1.143:5900 -N
```

Let's break this command down –

- ❖ ssh – Runs the local ssh utility
- ❖ -f – ssh should run in the background after the task fully executes
- ❖ rdc@192.168.1.143 – Remote ssh user on the CentOS server hosting VNC services
- ❖ -L 2200:192.168.1.143:5900 – Create our tunnel [Local Port]:[remote host]:[remote port of VNC service]
- ❖ -N tells ssh we do not wish to execute a command on the remote system

```
bash-3.2# ssh -f rdc@192.168.1.143 -L 2200:192.168.1.143:5900 -N
rdc@192.168.1.143's password:
```

After successfully entering the remote ssh user's password, our ssh tunnel is created. Now for the cool part! To connect we point our VNC client at the localhost on the port of our tunnel, in this case port 2200. Following is the configuration on Mac Laptop's VNC Client –

| Computer Info | Secure Connection | More Settings |

Name : `Local SSH Tunnel to Centos`

Address or Hostname : `localhost`

Port : `2200`

Operating System : `Linux`

Authentication

Authentication type : `VNC Password`

Password : `•••••••`

Cancel   Save

And finally, our remote VNC Desktop Connection!

The cool thing about SSH tunneling is it can be used for almost any protocol. SSH tunnels are commonly used to bypass egress and ingress port filtering by an ISP, as well as trick application layer IDS/IPS while evading other session layer monitoring.

❖ Your ISP may filter port 5900 for non-business accounts but allow SSH on port 22 (or one could run SSH on any port if port 22 is filtered).
❖ Application level IPS and IDS look at payload. For example, a common buffer overflow or SQL Injection. End-to-end SSH encryption will encrypt application layer data.

SSH Tunneling is great tool in a Linux Administrator's toolbox for getting things done. However, as an Administrator we want to explore locking down the availability of lesser privileged users having access to SSH tunneling.

Administration Security Note – Restricting SSH Tunneling is something that requires thought on the part of an Administrator. Assessing why users need SSH Tunneling in the first place; what users need tunneling; along with practical risk probability and worst-case impact.

This is an advanced topic stretching outside the realm of an intermediate level primer. Research on this topic is advised for those who wish to reach the upper echelons of CentOS Linux Administration.

Use SSH Tunnel for Remote X-Windows

The design of X-Windows in Linux is really neat compared to that of Windows. If we want to control a remote Linux box from another Linux boxm we can take advantage of mechanisms built into X.

X-Windows (often called just "X"), provides the mechanism to display application windows originating from one Linux box to the display portion of X on another Linux box. So through SSH we can request an X-Windows application be forwarded to the display of another Linux box across the world!

To run an X Application remotely via an ssh tunnel, we just need to run a single command −

```
[root@localhost]# ssh -X rdc@192.168.1.105
```

The syntax is − ssh -X [user]@[host], and the host must be running ssh with a valid user.

Following is a screenshot of GIMP running on a Ubuntu Workstation through a remote XWindows ssh tunnel.

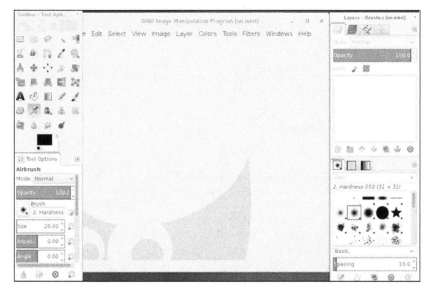

It is pretty simple to run applications remotely from another Linux server or workstation. It is also possible to start an entire X-Session and have the entire desktop environment remotely through a few methods.

- ❖ XDMCP
- ❖ Headless software packages such as NX
- ❖ Configuring alternate displays and desktops in X and desktop managers such as Gnome or KDE

This method is most commonly used for headless servers with no physical display and really exceeds the scope of an intermediate level primer. However, it is good to know of the options available.

LINUX ADMIN - TRAFFIC MONITORING IN CENTOS

There are several third party tools that can add enhanced capabilities for CentOS traffic monitoring. In this tutorial, we will focus on those that are packaged in the main CentOS distribution repositories and the Fedora EPEL repository.

There will always be situations where an Administrator (for one reason or another) is left with only tools in the main CentOS repositories. Most utilities discussed are designed to be used by an Administrator with the shell of physical access. When traffic monitoring with an accessible web-gui, using third party utilities such as ntop-ng or Nagios is the best choice (versus re-creating such facilities from scratch).

For further research on both configurable web-gui solutions, following are a few links to get started on research.

Traffic Monitoring for LAN / WAN Scenarios

Nagios

Nagios has been around for a long time, therefore, it is both tried and tested. At one point it was all free and open-source, but has since advanced into an Enterprise solution with paid licensing models to support the need of Enterprise sophistication. Hence, before planning any rollouts with Nagios, make sure the open-source licensed versions will meet your needs or plan on spending with an Enterprise Budget in mind.

Most open-source Nagios traffic monitoring software can be found at: https://www.nagios.org

For a summarized history of Nagious, here is the official Nagios History page: https://www.nagios.org/about/history/

ntopng

Another great tool allowing bandwidth and traffic monitoring via a web-gui is called ntopng. ntopng is similar to the Unix utility ntop, and can collect data for an entire LAN or WAN. Providing a web-gui for administration, configuration, and charting makes it easy to use for the entire IT Departments.

Like Nagious, ntopng has both open-source and paid enterprise versions available. For more information about ntopng, please visit the website: http://www.ntop.org/

Install Fedora EPEL Repository — Extra Packages for Enterprise Linux

To access some of the needed tools for traffic monitoring, we will need to configure our CentOS system to use the EPEL Repository.

The EPEL Repository is not officially maintained or supported by CentOS. However, it is maintained by a group of Fedora Core volunteers to address the packages commonly used by Enterprise Linux professionals not included in either CentOS, Fedora Core, or Red Hat Linux Enterprise.

Caution –

Remember, the EPEL Repository is not official for CentOS and may break compatibility and functionality on production servers with common dependencies. With that in mind, it is advised to always test on a non-production server running the same services as production before deploying on a system critical box.

Really, the biggest advantage of using the EHEL Repository over any other third party repository with CentOS is that we can be sure the binaries are not tainted. It is considered a best practice to not use the repositories from an untrusted source.

With all that said, the official EPEL Repository is so common with CentOS that it can be easily installed via YUM.

```
[root@CentOS rdc]# yum -y install epel-release
Loaded plugins: fastestmirror, langpacks
Loading mirror speeds from cached hostfile
* base: repo1.dal.innoscale.net
* extras: repo1.dal.innoscale.net
* updates: mirror.hmc.edu
Resolving Dependencies
 --> Running transaction check
 ---> Package epel-release.noarch 0:7-9 will be installed
 --> Finished Dependency Resolution
Dependencies Resolved
--{ condensed output }--
```

After installing the EPEL Repository, we will want to update it.

```
[root@CentOS rdc]# yum repolist
Loaded plugins: fastestmirror, langpacks
epel/x86_64/metalink
|  11 kB  00:00:00
epel
| 4.3 kB  00:00:00
(1/3): epel/x86_64/group_gz
| 170 kB  00:00:00
(2/3): epel/x86_64/updateinfo
| 753 kB  00:00:01
(3/3): epel/x86_64/primary_db
--{ condensed output }--
```

At this point, our EPEL repository should be configured and ready to use. Let's start by installing nload for interface bandwidth monitoring.

The tools we will focus on in this tutorial are –

- ❖ nload
- ❖ ntop
- ❖ ifstst
- ❖ iftop
- ❖ vnstat
- ❖ net hogs

❖ Wireshark
❖ TCP Dump
❖ Traceroute

These are all standard for monitoring traffic in Linux Enterprises. The usage of each range from simple to advanced, so we will only briefly discuss tools such as Wireshark and TCP Dump.

Install and Use nload

With our EPEL Repositories installed and configured in CentOS, we now should be able to install and use nload. This utility is designed to chart bandwidth per interface in real-time.

Like most other basic installs nload is installed via the YUM package manager.

```
[root@CentOS rdc]# yum -y install nload
Resolving Dependencies
--> Running transaction check
---> Package nload.x86_64 0:0.7.4-4.el7 will be installed
--> Finished Dependency Resolution
Dependencies Resolved
================================================================================
==========
================================================================================
==========

Package              Arch
Version              Repository          Size
================================================================================
==========
================================================================================
==========
Installing:
nload                x86_64
0.7.4-4.el7          epel                70 k
Transaction Summary
================================================================================
==========
================================================================================
==========
Install  1 Package
Total download size: 70 k
Installed size: 176 k
Downloading packages:
--{ condensed output }--
```

Now we have nload installed, and using it is pretty straight forward.

```
[root@CentOS rdc]# nload enp0s5
```

nload will monitor the specified interface. In this case, enp0s5 an Ethernet interface, in real-time from the terminal for network traffic loads and total bandwidth usage.

```
File  Edit  View  Search  Terminal  Help
Device lo [127.0.0.1] (1/2):
================================================================
Incoming:                              Outgoing:
Curr: 0.00 kByte/s                     Curr: 0.00 kByte/s
Avg: 0.00 kByte/s                      Avg: 0.00 kByte/s
Min: 0.00 kByte/s                      Min: 0.00 kByte/s
Max: 0.00 kByte/s                      Max: 0.00 kByte/s
Ttl: 0.00 MByte                        Ttl: 0.00 MByte

Device enp0s5 [10.211.55.1] (2/2):
================================================================
Incoming:                              Outgoing:
Curr: 0.00 kByte/s                     Curr: 0.00 kByte/s
Avg: 0.21 kByte/s                      Avg: 0.55 kByte/s
Min: 0.00 kByte/s                      Min: 0.00 kByte/s
Max: 1.14 kByte/s                      Max: 5.68 kByte/s
Ttl: 34.45 MByte                       Ttl: 5.59 MByte
```

As seen, nload will chart both incoming and outgoing data from the specified interface, along with providing a physical representation of the data flow with hash marks "#".

The depicted screenshot is of a simple webpage being loaded with some background daemon traffic.

Common command line switches for nload are −

Command	Action
-a	Time period
-t	Time update interval in milliseconds, the default is 500
-u	Sets display of traffic measurement h
-U	Sets total in/out traffic measurement units same options as -u

The standard syntax for nload is −

nload [options] <interface>

If no interface is specified, nload will automatically grab the first Ethernet interface. Let's try measuring the total data in/out in Megabytes and current data-transfer speeds in Megabits.

[root@CentOS rdc]# nload -U M -u m

```
                                    rdc@CentOS:/home/rdc                           _  □  ×
File  Edit  View  Search  Terminal  Help
Device enp0s5 [10.211.55.1] (1/4):
========================================================================================
Incoming:



                                                              Curr: 0.00 MBit/s
                                                              Avg: 0.34 MBit/s
                                         #|                   Min: 0.00 MBit/s
                                  ##      ##                  Max: 2.89 MBit/s
                                  ##     .##                  Ttl: 30.37 MByte
                           ..   .. ##.####    ..    ..
Outgoing:



                                                              Curr: 0.00 MBit/s
                                                              Avg: 0.00 MBit/s
                                                              Min: 0.00 MBit/s
                                                              Max: 0.67 MBit/s
                           ..    .|.  .  .                    Ttl: 4.21 MByte
```

Data coming in/out the current interface is measured in megabits per second and each "Ttl" row, representing total data in/out is displayed in Megabytes.

nload is useful for an administrator to see how much data has passed through an interface and how much data is currently coming in/out a specified interface.

To see other interfaces without closing nload, simply use the left/right arrow keys. This will cycle through all available interfaces on the system.

It is possible to monitor multiple interfaces simultaneously using the -m switch –

```
[root@CentOS rdc]# nload -u K -U M -m lo -m enp0s5
```

load monitoring two interfaces simultaneously (lo and enp0s5) –

```
File  Edit  View  Search  Terminal  Help
Device lo [127.0.0.1] (1/2):
========================================================================================
Incoming:                                    Outgoing:
Curr: 0.00 kByte/s                           Curr: 0.00 kByte/s
Avg: 0.00 kByte/s                            Avg: 0.00 kByte/s
Min: 0.00 kByte/s                            Min: 0.00 kByte/s
Max: 0.00 kByte/s                            Max: 0.00 kByte/s
Ttl: 0.00 MByte                              Ttl: 0.00 MByte

Device enp0s5 [10.211.55.1] (2/2):
========================================================================================
Incoming:                                    Outgoing:
Curr: 0.00 kByte/s                           Curr: 0.00 kByte/s
Avg: 0.21 kByte/s                            Avg: 0.55 kByte/s
Min: 0.00 kByte/s                            Min: 0.00 kByte/s
Max: 1.14 kByte/s                            Max: 5.68 kByte/s
Ttl: 34.45 MByte                             Ttl: 5.59 MByte
```

LINUX ADMIN - LOG MANAGEMENT

systemd has changed the way system logging is managed for CentOS Linux. Instead of every daemon on the system placing logs into individual locations than using tools such as tail or grep as the primary way of sorting and filtering log entries, journald has brought a single point of administration to analyzing system logs.

The main components behind systemd logging are: journal, jounralctl, and journald.conf

journald is the main logging daemon and is configured by editing journald.conf while journalctl is used to analyze events logged by journald.

Events logged by journald include: kernel events, user processes, and daemon services.

Set the Correct System Time Zone

Before using journalctl, we need to make sure our system time is set to the correct time. To do this, we want to use timedatectl.

Let's check the current system time.

```
[root@centos rdc]# timedatectl status
Local time: Mon 2017-03-20 00:14:49 MDT
Universal time: Mon 2017-03-20 06:14:49 UTC
RTC time: Mon 2017-03-20 06:14:49
Time zone: America/Denver (MDT, -0600)
NTP enabled: yes
NTP synchronized: yes
RTC in local TZ: no
DST active: yes
Last DST change: DST began at
        Sun 2017-03-12 01:59:59 MST
        Sun 2017-03-12 03:00:00 MDT
Next DST change: DST ends (the clock jumps one hour backwards) at
        Sun 2017-11-05 01:59:59 MDT
        Sun 2017-11-05 01:00:00 MST
        [root@centos rdc]#
```

Currently, the system is correct to the local time zone. If your system is not, let's set the correct time zone. After changing the settings, CentOS will automatically calculate the time zone offset from the current time zone, adjusting the system clock right away.

Let's list all the time zones with timedatectl —

```
[root@centos rdc]# timedatectl list-timezones
Africa/Abidjan
Africa/Accra
Africa/Addis_Ababa
Africa/Algiers
Africa/Asmara
Africa/Bamako
Africa/Bangui
```

Africa/Banjul
Africa/Bissau

That is the contended output from timedatectl list-timezones. To find a specific local time-zone, the grep command can be used −

```
[root@centos rdc]# timedatectl list-timezones | grep -i "america/New_York"
America/New_York
[root@centos rdc]#
```

The label used by CentOS is usually Country/Region with an underscore instead of space (New_York versus "New York").

Now let's set our time zone −

```
[root@centos rdc]# timedatectl set-timezone "America/New_York"
[root@centos rdc]# date
Mon Mar 20 02:28:44 EDT 2017
[root@centos rdc]#
```

Your system clock should automatically adjust the time.

Use journalctl to Analyze Logs

Common command line switches when using journalctl −

Switch	Action
-k	Lists only kernel messages
-u	Lists by specific unit (httpd, sshd, etc...)
-b	Boots the label offset
-o	Logs the output format
-p	Filters by log type (either name or number)
-F	Fieldname or fieldnamevalue
--utc	Time in UTC offset
--since	Filter by timeframe

Examine Boot Logs

First, we will examine and configure the boot logs in CentOS Linux. The first thing you will notice is that CentOS, by default, doesn't store boot logging that is persistent across reboots.

To check boot logs per reboot instance, we can issue the following command −

```
[root@centos rdc]# journalctl --list-boots
-4 bca6380a31a2463aa60ba551698455b5 Sun 2017-03-19 22:01:57 MDT—Sun 2017-03-19 22:11:02 MDT
-3 3aaa9b84f9504fa1a68db5b49c0c7208 Sun 2017-03-19 22:11:09 MDT—Sun 2017-03-19 22:15:03 MDT
-2 f80b231272bf48ffb1d2ce9f758c5a5f Sun 2017-03-19 22:15:11 MDT—Sun 2017-03-19 22:54:06 MDT
-1 a071c1eed09d4582a870c13be5984ed6 Sun 2017-03-19 22:54:26 MDT—Mon 2017-03-20 00:48:29 MDT
 0 9b4e6cdb43b14a328b1fa6448bb72a56 Mon 2017-03-20 00:48:38 MDT—Mon 2017-03-20 01:07:36 MDT
```

After rebooting the system, we can see another entry.

```
[root@centos rdc]# journalctl --list-boots
-5 bca6380a31a2463aa60ba551698455b5 Sun 2017-03-19 22:01:57 MDT—Sun 2017-03-19 22:11:02 MDT
-4 3aaa9b84f9504fa1a68db5b49c0c7208 Sun 2017-03-19 22:11:09 MDT—Sun 2017-03-19 22:15:03 MDT
-3 f80b231272bf48ffb1d2ce9f758c5a5f Sun 2017-03-19 22:15:11 MDT—Sun 2017-03-19 22:54:06 MDT
```

```
-2 a071c1eed09d4582a870c13be5984ed6 Sun 2017-03-19 22:54:26 MDT—Mon 2017-03-20 00:48:29 MDT
-1 9b4e6cdb43b14a328b1fa6448bb72a56 Mon 2017-03-20 00:48:38 MDT—Mon 2017-03-20 01:09:57 MDT
 0 aa6aaf0f0f0d4fcf924e17849593d972 Mon 2017-03-20 01:10:07 MDT—Mon 2017-03-20 01:12:44 MDT
```

Now, let's examine the last boot logging instance –

```
root@centos rdc]# journalctl -b -5
-- Logs begin at Sun 2017-03-19 22:01:57 MDT, end at Mon 2017-03-20 01:20:27 MDT. --
Mar 19 22:01:57 localhost.localdomain systemd-journal[97]: Runtime journal is using 8.0M
(max allowed 108.4M
Mar 19 22:01:57 localhost.localdomain kernel: Initializing cgroup subsys cpuset
Mar 19 22:01:57 localhost.localdomain kernel: Initializing cgroup subsys cpu
Mar 19 22:01:57 localhost.localdomain kernel: Initializing cgroup subsys cpuacct
Mar 19 22:01:57 localhost.localdomain kernel: Linux version 3.10.0514.6.2.el7.x86_64
(builder@kbuilder.dev.
Mar 19 22:01:57 localhost.localdomain kernel: Command line:
BOOT_IMAGE=/vmlinuz-3.10.0-514.6.2.el7.x86_64 ro
Mar 19 22:01:57 localhost.localdomain kernel: Disabled fast string operations
Mar 19 22:01:57 localhost.localdomain kernel: e820: BIOS-provided physical RAM map:
```

Above is the condensed output from our last boot. We could also refer back to a boot log from hours, days, weeks, months, and even years. However, by default CentOS doesn't store persistent boot logs. To enable persistently storing boot logs, we need to make a few configuration changes –

- ❖ Make central storage points for boot logs
- ❖ Give proper permissions to a new log folder
- ❖ Configure journald.conf for persistent logging

Configure Boot Location for Persistent Boot Logs

The initial place journald will want to store persistent boot logs is /var/log/journal. Since this doesn't exist by default, let's create it –

```
[root@centos rdc]# mkdir /var/log/journal
```

Now, let's give the directory proper permissions journald daemon access –

```
systemd-tmpfiles --create --prefix /var/log/journal
```

Finally, let's tell journald it should store persistent boot logs. In vim or your favorite text editor, open /etc/systemd/jounrald.conf".

```
# See journald.conf(5) for details.
[Journal]=Storage=peristent
```

The line we are concerned with is, Storage=. First remove the comment #, then change to Storage = persistent as depicted above. Save and reboot your CentOS system and take care that there should be multiple entries when running journalctl list-boots.

Note – A constantly changing machine-id like that from a VPS provider can cause journald to fail at storing persistent boot logs. There are many workarounds for such a scenario. It is best to peruse the current fixes posted to CentOS Admin forums, than follow the trusted advice from those who have found plausible VPS workarounds.

To examine a specific boot log, we simply need to get each offset using journald --list-boots the offset with the -b switch. So to check the second boot log we'd use –

```
journalctl -b -2
```

The default for -b with no boot log offset specified will always be the current boot log after the last reboot.

Analyze Logs by Log Type

Events from journald are numbered and categorized into 7 separate types –

```
0 - emerg   :: System is unusable
1 - alert   :: Action must be taken immediatly
2 - crit    :: Action is advised to be taken immediatly
3 - err     :: Error effecting functionality of application
4 - warning :: Usually means a common issue that can affect security or usilbity
5 - info    :: logged informtation for common operations
6 - debug   :: usually disabled by default to troubleshoot functionality
```

Hence, if we want to see all warnings the following command can be issued via journalctl –

```
[root@centos rdc]# journalctl -p 4
-- Logs begin at Sun 2017-03-19 22:01:57 MDT, end at Wed 2017-03-22 22:33:42 MDT. --
Mar 19 22:01:57 localhost.localdomain kernel: ACPI: RSDP 00000000000f6a10 00024
(v02 PTLTD )
Mar 19 22:01:57 localhost.localdomain kernel: ACPI: XSDT 0000000095eea65b 0005C
(v01 INTEL 440BX   06040000 VMW  01
Mar 19 22:01:57 localhost.localdomain kernel: ACPI: FACP 0000000095efee73 000F4
(v04 INTEL 440BX   06040000 PTL  00
Mar 19 22:01:57 localhost.localdomain kernel: ACPI: DSDT 0000000095eec749 1272A
(v01 PTLTD Custom   06040000 MSFT 03
Mar 19 22:01:57 localhost.localdomain kernel: ACPI: FACS 0000000095efffc0 00040
Mar 19 22:01:57 localhost.localdomain kernel: ACPI: BOOT 0000000095eec721 00028
(v01 PTLTD $SBFTBL$ 06040000 LTP 00
Mar 19 22:01:57 localhost.localdomain kernel: ACPI: APIC 0000000095eeb8bd 00742
(v01 PTLTD ? APIC  06040000 LTP 00
Mar 19 22:01:57 localhost.localdomain kernel: ACPI: MCFG 0000000095eeb881 0003C
(v01 PTLTD $PCITBL$ 06040000 LTP 00
Mar 19 22:01:57 localhost.localdomain kernel: ACPI: SRAT 0000000095eea757 008A8
(v02 VMWARE MEMPLUG 06040000 VMW  00
Mar 19 22:01:57 localhost.localdomain kernel: ACPI: HPET 0000000095eea71f 00038
(v01 VMWARE VMW HPET 06040000 VMW  00
Mar 19 22:01:57 localhost.localdomain kernel: ACPI: WAET 0000000095eea6f7 00028
(v01 VMWARE VMW WAET 06040000 VMW  00
Mar 19 22:01:57 localhost.localdomain kernel: Zone ranges:
Mar 19 22:01:57 localhost.localdomain kernel:   DMA      [mem 0x000010000x00ffffff]
Mar 19 22:01:57 localhost.localdomain kernel:   DMA32    [mem 0x010000000xffffffff]
Mar 19 22:01:57 localhost.localdomain kernel:   Normal   empty
Mar 19 22:01:57 localhost.localdomain kernel: Movable zone start for each node
Mar 19 22:01:57 localhost.localdomain kernel: Early memory node ranges
Mar 19 22:01:57 localhost.localdomain kernel:   node  0: [mem 0x000010000x0009dfff]
Mar 19 22:01:57 localhost.localdomain kernel:   node  0: [mem 0x001000000x95edffff]
Mar 19 22:01:57 localhost.localdomain kernel:   node  0: [mem 0x95f000000x95ffffff]
Mar 19 22:01:57 localhost.localdomain kernel: Built 1 zonelists in Node order,
mobility grouping on. Total pages: 60
Mar 19 22:01:57 localhost.localdomain kernel: Policy zone: DMA32
Mar 19 22:01:57 localhost.localdomain kernel: ENERGY_PERF_BIAS: Set to
'normal', was 'performance'
```

The above shows all warnings for the past 4 days on the system.

The new way of viewing and perusing logs with systemd does take little practice and research to become familiar with. However, with different output formats and particular notice to making all packaged daemon logs universal, it is worth embracing. journald offers great flexibility and efficiency over traditional log analysis methods.

LINUX ADMIN - BACKUP AND RECOVERY

Before exploring methods particular to CentOS for deploying a standard backup plan, let's first discuss typical considerations for a standard level backup policy. The first thing we want to get accustomed to is the 3-2-1 backup rule.

3-2-1 Backup Strategy

Throughout the industry, you'll often hear the term 3-2-1 backup model. This is a very good approach to live by when implementing a backup plan. 3-2-1 is defined as follows: 3 copies of data; for example, we may have the working copy; a copy put onto the CentOS server designed for redundancy using rsync; and rotated, offsite USB backups are made from data on the backup server. 2 different backup mediums. We would actually have three different backup mediums in this case: the working copy on an SSD of a laptop or workstation, the CentOS server data on a RADI6 Array, and the offsite backups put on USB drives. 1 copy of data offsite; we are rotating the USB drives offsite on a nightly basis. Another modern approach may be a cloud backup provider.

System Recovery

A bare metal restore plan is simply a plan laid out by a CentOS administrator to get vital systems online with all data intact. Assuming 100% systems failure and loss of all past system hardware, an administrator must have a plan to achieve uptime with intact user-data costing minimal downtime. The monolithic kernel used in Linux actually makes bare metal restores using system images much easier than Windows. Where Windows uses a micro-kernel architecture.

A full data restore and bare metal recovery are usually accomplished through a combination of methods including working, configured production disk-images of key operational servers, redundant backups of user data abiding by the 3-2-1 rule. Even some sensitive files that may be stored in a secure, fireproof safe with limited access to the trusted company personnel.

A multiphase bare metal restore and data recovery plan using native CentOS tools may consist of −

- ❖ dd to make and restore production disk-images of configured servers
- ❖ rsync to make incremental backups of all user data
- ❖ tar & gzip to store encrypted backups of files with passwords and notes from administrators. Commonly, this can be put on a USB drive, encrypted and locked in a safe that a Senior Manager access. Also, this ensures someone else will know vital security credentials if the current administrator wins the lottery and disappears to a sunny island somewhere.

If a system crashes due to a hardware failure or disaster, following will be the different phases of restoring operations −

- ❖ Build a working server with a configured bare metal image
- ❖ Restore data to the working server from backups
- ❖ Have physical access to credentials needed to perform the first two operations

Use rsync for File Level Backups

rsync is a great utility for syncing directories of files either locally or to another server. rsync has been used for years by System Administrators, hence it is very refined for the purpose of backing up data. In the author's opinion, one of the best features of sync is its ability to be scripted from the command line.

In this tutorial, we will discuss rsync in various ways −

- ❖ Explore and talk about some common options
- ❖ Create local backups
- ❖ Create remote backups over SSH
- ❖ Restore local backups

rsync is named for its purpose: Remote Sync and is both powerful and flexible in use.

Following is a basic rsync remote backup over ssh −

```
MiNi:~ rdc$ rsync -aAvz --progress ./Desktop/ImportantStuff/
rdc@192.168.1.143:home/rdc/ Documents/RemoteStuff/
rdc@192.168.1.143's password:
sending incremental file list
  6,148 100%   0.00kB/s   0:00:00 (xfr#1, to-chk=23/25)
2017-02-14 16_26_47-002 - Veeam_Architecture001.png
  33,144 100%   31.61MB/s   0:00:00 (xfr#2, to-chk=22/25)
A Guide to the WordPress REST API | Toptal.pdf
  892,406 100%   25.03MB/s   0:00:00 (xfr#3, to-chk=21/25)
Rick Cardon Technologies, LLC..webloc
  77 100%   2.21kB/s   0:00:00 (xfr#4, to-chk=20/25)
backbox-4.5.1-i386.iso
  43,188,224 1%   4.26MB/s   0:08:29
sent 2,318,683,608 bytes received 446 bytes 7,302,941.90 bytes/sec
total size is 2,327,091,863 speedup is 1.00
MiNi:~ rdc$
```

The following sync sent nearly 2.3GB of data across our LAN. The beauty of rsync is it works incrementally at the block level on a file-by-file basis. This means, if we change just two characters in a 1MB text file, only one or two blocks will be transferred across the lan on the next sync!

Furthermore, the incremental function can be disabled in favor of more network bandwidth used for less CPU utilization. This might prove advisable if constantly copying several 10MB database files every 10 minutes on a 1Gb dedicated Backup-Lan. The reasoning is: these will always be changing and will be transmitting incrementally every 10 minutes and may tax load of the remote CPU. Since the total transfer load will not exceed 5 minutes, we may just wish to sync the database files in their entirety.

Following are the most common switches with rsync −

rsync syntax:
rsync [options] [local path] [[remote host:remote path] or [target path

Switch	Action
-a	Archive mode and assumes -r, -p, -t, -g, -l
-d	Sync only directory tree, no files
-r	Recursive into directory
-l	Copy symlinks as symlinks
-p	Preserve permissions
-g	Preserve group
-v	Verbose output
-z	Compress over network link
-X	Preserve extended attributes
-A	Preserve ACLs
-t	Preserve timestamps
-W	Transfer whole file, not incremental blocks
-u	Do not overwrite files on target
--progress	Show transfer progress
--delete	Delete older files on target
--max-size = XXX	Max file size to sync

When to use rsync

My personal preference for rsync is when backing up files from a source host to a target host. For example, all the home directories for data recovery or even offsite and into the cloud for disaster recovery.

Local Backup With rsync

We have already seen how to transfer files from one host to another. The same method can be used to sync directories and files locally.

Let's make a manual incremental backup of /etc/ in our root user's directory.

First, we need to create a directory off ~/root for the synced backup −

```
[root@localhost rdc]# mkdir /root/etc_baks
```

Then, assure there is enough free disk-space.

```
[root@localhost rdc]# du -h --summarize /etc/
49M   /etc/

[root@localhost rdc]# df -h
Filesystem          Size   Used   Avail   Use%   Mounted on
/dev/mapper/cl-root  43G    15G    28G     35%    /
```

We are good for syncing our entire /etc/ directory −

```
rsync -aAvr /etc/ /root/etc_baks/
```

Our synced /etc/ directory –

```
[root@localhost etc_baks]# ls -l ./
total 1436
drwxr-xr-x.  3 root root     101 Feb  1 19:40 abrt
-rw-r--r--.  1 root root      16 Feb  1 19:51 adjtime
-rw-r--r--.  1 root root    1518 Jun  7 2013 aliases
-rw-r--r--.  1 root root   12288 Feb 27 19:06 aliases.db
drwxr-xr-x.  2 root root      51 Feb  1 19:41 alsa
drwxr-xr-x.  2 root root    4096 Feb 27 17:11 alternatives
-rw-------.  1 root root     541 Mar 31 2016 anacrontab
-rw-r--r--.  1 root root      55 Nov  4 12:29 asound.conf
-rw-r--r--.  1 root root       1 Nov  5 14:16 at.deny
drwxr-xr-x.  2 root root      32 Feb  1 19:40 at-spi2
--{ condensed output }--
```

Now let's do an incremental rsync –

```
[root@localhost etc_baks]# rsync -aAvr --progress /etc/ /root/etc_baks/
sending incremental file list
test_incremental.txt
    0 100%    0.00kB/s    0:00:00 (xfer#1, to-check=1145/1282)
sent 204620 bytes  received 2321 bytes  413882.00 bytes/sec
total size is 80245040  speedup is 387.77
[root@localhost etc_baks]#
```

Only our test_incremental.txt file was copied.

Remote Differential Backups With rsync

Let's do our initial rsync full backup onto a server with a backup plan deployed. This example is actually backing up a folder on a Mac OS X Workstation to a CentOS server. Another great aspect of rsync is that it can be used on any platform rsync has been ported to.

```
MiNi:~ rdc$ rsync -aAvz Desktop/ImportanStuff/
rdc@192.168.1.143:Documents/RemoteStuff
rdc@192.168.1.143's password:
sending incremental file list
./
A Guide to the WordPress REST API | Toptal.pdf
Rick Cardon Tech LLC.webloc
VeeamDiagram.png
backbox-4.5.1-i386.iso
dhcp_admin_script_update.py
DDWRT/
DDWRT/.DS_Store
DDWRT/ddwrt-linksys-wrt1200acv2-webflash.bin
DDWRT/ddwrt_mod_notes.docx
DDWRT/factory-to-ddwrt.bin
open_ldap_config_notes/
open_ldap_config_notes/ldap_directory_a.png
open_ldap_config_notes/open_ldap_notes.txt
perl_scripts/
perl_scripts/mysnmp.pl
php_scripts/
php_scripts/chunked.php
php_scripts/gettingURL.php
sent 2,318,281,023 bytes  received 336 bytes  9,720,257.27 bytes/sec
total size is 2,326,636,892  speedup is 1.00
MiNi:~ rdc$
```

We have now backed up a folder from a workstation onto a server running a RAID6 volume with rotated disaster recovery media stored offsite. Using rsync has given us standard 3-2-1 backup with only one server having an expensive redundant disk array and rotated differential backups.

Now let's do another backup of the same folder using rsync after a single new file named test_file.txt has been added.

```
MiNi:~ rdc$ rsync -aAvz Desktop/ImportanStuff/
rdc@192.168.1.143:Documents/RemoteStuff
rdc@192.168.1.143's password:
sending incremental file list
./
test_file.txt
sent 814 bytes  received 61 bytes  134.62 bytes/sec
total size is 2,326,636,910  speedup is 2,659,013.61
MiNi:~ rdc$
```

As you can see, only the new file was delivered to the server via rsync. The differential comparison was made on a file-by-file basis.

A few things to note are: This only copies the new file: test_file.txt, since it was the only file with changes. rsync uses ssh. We did not ever need to use our root account on either machine.

Simple, powerful and effective, rsync is great for backing up entire folders and directory structures. However, rsync by itself doesn't automate the process. This is where we need to dig into our toolbox and find the best, small, and simple tool for the job.

To automate rsync backups with cronjobs, it is essential that SSH users be set up using SSH keys for authentication. This combined with cronjobs enables rsync to be done automatically at timed intervals.

Use DD for Block-by-Block Bare Metal Recovery Images

DD is a Linux utility that has been around since the dawn of the Linux kernel meeting the GNU Utilities.

dd in simplest terms copies an image of a selected disk area. Then provides the ability to copy selected blocks of a physical disk. So unless you have backups, once dd writes over a disk, all blocks are replaced. Loss of previous data exceeds the recovery capabilities for even highly priced professional-level data-recovery.

The entire process for making a bootable system image with dd is as follows −

- ❖ Boot from the CentOS server with a bootable linux distribution
- ❖ Find the designation of the bootable disk to be imaged
- ❖ Decide location where the recovery image will be stored
- ❖ Find the block size used on your disk
- ❖ Start the dd image operation

In this tutorial, for the sake of time and simplicity, we will be creating an ISO image of the master-boot record from a CentOS virtual machine. We will then store this image offsite. In case our MBR becomes corrupted and needs to be restored, the same process can be applied to an entire bootable disk or partition. However, the time and disk space needed really goes a little overboard for this tutorial.

It is encouraged for CentOS admins to become proficient in restoring a fully bootable disk/partition in a test environment and perform a bare metal restore. This will take a lot of pressure off when eventually one needs to complete the practice in a real life situation with Managers and a few dozen end-users counting downtime. In such a case, 10 minutes of figuring things out can seem like an eternity and make one sweat.

Note – When using dd make sure to NOT confuse source and target volumes. You can destroy data and bootable servers by copying your backup location to a boot drive. Or possibly worse destroy data forever by copying over data at a very low level with DD.

Following are the common command line switches and parameters for dd –

Switch	Action
if=	In file or source to be copied
of=	Out file or the copy of the in file
bs	Set both input and output block size
obs	Set output file block size
ibs	Set input file block size
count	Set the number of blocks to copy
conv	Extra options to add for imaging
Noerror	Do not stop processing an error
sync	Pads unfitted input blocks in the event of error or misalignment

Note on block size – The default block size for dd is 512 bytes. This was the standard block size of lower density hard disk drives. Today's higher density HDDs have increased to 4096 byte (4kB) block sizes to allow for disks ranging from 1TB and larger. Thus, we will want to check disk block size before using dd with newer, higher capacity hard disks.

For this tutorial, instead of working on a production server with dd, we will be using a CentOS installation running in VMWare. We will also configure VMWare to boot a bootable Linux ISO image instead of working with a bootable USB Stick.

First, we will need to download the CentOS image entitled: CentOS Gnome ISO. This is almost 3GB and it is advised to always keep a copy for creating bootable USB thumb-drives and booting into virtual server installations for trouble-shooting and bare metal images.

Other bootable Linux distros will work just as well. Linux Mint can be used for bootable ISOs as it has great hardware support and polished GUI disk tools for maintenance.

CentOS GNOME Live bootable image can be downloaded from: http://buildlogs.centos.org/rolling/7/isos/x86_64/CentOS-7-x86_64-LiveGNOME.iso

Let's configure our VMWare Workstation installation to boot from our Linux bootable image. The steps are for VMWare on OS X. However, they are similar across VMWare Workstation on Linux, Windows, and even Virtual Box.

Note – Using a virtual desktop solution like Virtual Box or VMWare Workstation is a great way to set up lab scenarios for learning CentOS Administration tasks. It provides the ability to install several CentOS installations, practically no hardware configuration letting the person focus on administration, and even save the server state before making changes.

First let's configure a virtual cd-rom and attach our ISO image to boot instead of the virtual CentOS server installation –

```
cd001
cd002
```

Now, set the startup disk –

```
cd003
cd004
```

Now when booted, our virtual machine will boot from the CentOS bootable ISO image and allow access to files on the Virtual CentOS server that was previously configured.

Let's check our disks to see where we want to copy the MBR from (condensed output is as follows).

```
MiNt ~ # fdisk -l
Disk /dev/sda: 60 GiB, 21474836480 bytes, 41943040 sectors
Units: sectors of 1 * 512 = 512 bytes
Sector size (logical/physical): 512 bytes / 512 bytes
I/O size (minimum/optimal): 512 bytes / 512 bytes
Disk /dev/sdb: 20 GiB, 21474836480 bytes, 41943040 sectors
Units: sectors of 1 * 512 = 512 bytes
Sector size (logical/physical): 512 bytes / 512 bytes
I/O size (minimum/optimal): 512 bytes / 512 bytes
```

We have located both our physical disks: sda and sdb. Each has a block size of 512 bytes. So, we will now run the dd command to copy the first 512 bytes for our MBR on SDA1.

The best way to do this is –

```
[root@mint rdc]# dd if=/dev/sda bs=512 count=1 | gzip -c >
/mnt/sdb/images/mbr.iso.gz
1+0 records in
1+0 records out
512 bytes copied, 0.000171388 s, 3.0 MB/s
[root@mint rdc]# ls /mnt/sdb/
```

```
mbr-iso.gz
```

```
[root@mint rdc]#
```

Just like that, we have full image of out master boot record. If we have enough room to image the boot drive, we could just as easily make a full system boot image −

```
dd if=/dev/INPUT/DEVICE-NAME-HERE conv=sync,noerror bs=4K | gzip -c >
/mnt/sdb/boot-server-centos-image.iso.gz
```

The conv=sync is used when bytes must be aligned for a physical medium. In this case, dd may get an error if exact 4K alignments are not read (say... a file that is only 3K but needs to take minimum of a single 4K block on disk. Or, there is simply an error reading and the file cannot be read by dd.). Thus, dd with conv=sync,noerror will pad the 3K with trivial, but useful data to physical medium in 4K block alignments. While not presenting an error that may end a large operation.

When working with data from disks we always want to include: conv=sync,noerror parameter.

This is simply because the disks are not streams like TCP data. They are made up of blocks aligned to a certain size. For example, if we have 512 byte blocks, a file of only 300 bytes still needs a full 512 bytes of disk-space (possibly 2 blocks for inode information like permissions and other filesystem information).

Use gzip and tar for Secure Storage

gzip and tar are two utilities a CentOS administrator must become accustomed to using. They are used for a lot more than to simply decompress archives.

Using Gnu Tar in CentOS Linux

Tar is an archiving utility similar to winrar on Windows. Its name Tape Archive abbreviated as tar pretty much sums up the utility. tar will take files and place them into an archive for logical convenience. Hence, instead of the dozens of files stored in /etc. we could just "tar" them up into an archive for backup and storage convenience.

tar has been the standard for storing archived files on Unix and Linux for many years. Hence, using tar along with gzip or bzip is considered as a best practice for archives on each system.

Following is a list of common command line switches and options used with tar −

Switch	Action
-c	Creates a new .tar archive
-C	Extracts to a different directory
-j	Uses bzip2 compression
-z	Uses gzip compression

-v	Verbose show archiving progress
-t	Lists archive contents
-f	File name of the archive
-x	Extracts tar archive

Following is the basic syntax for creating a tar archive.

```
tar -cvf [tar archive name]
```

Note on Compression mechanisms with tar – It is advised to stick with one of two common compression schemes when using tar: gzip and bzip2. gzip files consume less CPU resources but are usually larger in size. While bzip2 will take longer to compress, they utilize more CPU resources; but will result in a smaller end filesize.

When using file compression, we will always want to use standard file extensions letting everyone including ourselves know (versus guess by trial and error) what compression scheme is needed to extract archives.

bzip2	.tbz
bzip2	.tar.tbz
bzip2	.tb2
gzip	.tar.gz
gzip	.tgz

When needing to possibly extract archives on a Windows box or for use on Windows, it is advised to use the .tar.tbz or .tar.gz as most the three character single extensions will confuse Windows and Windows only Administrators (however, that is sometimes the desired outcome)

Let's create a gzipped tar archive from our remote backups copied from the Mac Workstation –

```
[rdc@mint Documents]$ tar -cvz -f RemoteStuff.tgz ./RemoteStuff/
./RemoteStuff/
./RemoteStuff/.DS_Store
./RemoteStuff/DDWRT/
./RemoteStuff/DDWRT/.DS_Store
./RemoteStuff/DDWRT/ddwrt-linksys-wrt1200acv2-webflash.bin
./RemoteStuff/DDWRT/ddwrt_mod_notes.docx
./RemoteStuff/DDWRT/factory-to-ddwrt.bin
./RemoteStuff/open_ldap_config_notes/
./RemoteStuff/open_ldap_config_notes/ldap_directory_a.png
./RemoteStuff/open_ldap_config_notes/open_ldap_notes.txt
./RemoteStuff/perl_scripts/
./RemoteStuff/perl_scripts/mysnmp.pl
./RemoteStuff/php_scripts/
./RemoteStuff/php_scripts/chunked.php
./RemoteStuff/php_scripts/gettingURL.php
./RemoteStuff/A Guide to the WordPress REST API | Toptal.pdf
./RemoteStuff/Rick Cardon Tech LLC.webloc
./RemoteStuff/VeeamDiagram.png
./RemoteStuff/backbox-4.5.1-i386.iso
./RemoteStuff/dhcp_admin_script_update.py
./RemoteStuff/test_file.txt
[rdc@mint Documents]$ ls -ld RemoteStuff.tgz
-rw-rw-r--. 1 rdc rdc 2317140451 Mar 12 06:10 RemoteStuff.tgz
```

Note – Instead of adding all the files directly to the archive, we archived the entire folder RemoteStuff. This is the easiest method. Simply because when extracted, the entire directory RemoteStuff is extracted with all the files inside the current working directory as ./currentWorkingDirectory/RemoteStuff/

Now let's extract the archive inside the /root/ home directory.

```
[root@centos ~]# tar -zxvf RemoteStuff.tgz
./RemoteStuff/
./RemoteStuff/.DS_Store
./RemoteStuff/DDWRT/
./RemoteStuff/DDWRT/.DS_Store
./RemoteStuff/DDWRT/ddwrt-linksys-wrt1200acv2-webflash.bin
./RemoteStuff/DDWRT/ddwrt_mod_notes.docx
./RemoteStuff/DDWRT/factory-to-ddwrt.bin
./RemoteStuff/open_ldap_config_notes/
./RemoteStuff/open_ldap_config_notes/ldap_directory_a.png
./RemoteStuff/open_ldap_config_notes/open_ldap_notes.txt
./RemoteStuff/perl_scripts/
./RemoteStuff/perl_scripts/mysnmp.pl
./RemoteStuff/php_scripts/
./RemoteStuff/php_scripts/chunked.php
./RemoteStuff/php_scripts/gettingURL.php
./RemoteStuff/A Guide to the WordPress REST API | Toptal.pdf
./RemoteStuff/Rick Cardon Tech LLC.webloc
./RemoteStuff/VeeamDiagram.png
./RemoteStuff/backbox-4.5.1-i386.iso
./RemoteStuff/dhcp_admin_script_update.py
./RemoteStuff/test_file.txt
[root@mint ~]# ping www.google.com
```

As seen above, all the files were simply extracted into the containing directory within our current working directory.

```
[root@centos ~]# ls -l
total 2262872
-rw-------. 1 root root       1752 Feb  1 19:52 anaconda-ks.cfg
drwxr-xr-x. 137 root root     8192 Mar  9 04:42 etc_baks
-rw-r--r--. 1 root root       1800 Feb  2 03:14 initial-setup-ks.cfg
drwxr-xr-x. 6 rdc  rdc        4096 Mar 10 22:20 RemoteStuff
-rw-r--r--. 1 root root 2317140451 Mar 12 07:12 RemoteStuff.tgz
-rw-r--r--. 1 root root       9446 Feb 25 05:09 ssl.conf [root@centos ~]#
```

Use gzip to Compress File Backups

As noted earlier, we can use either bzip2 or gzip from tar with the -j or -z command line switches. We can also use gzip to compress individual files. However, using bzip or gzip alone does not offer as many features as when combined with tar.

When using gzip, the default action is to remove the original files, replacing each with a compressed version adding the .gz extension.

Some common command line switches for gzip are –

Switch	Action
-c	Keeps files after placing into the archive
-l	Get statistics for the compressed archive
-r	Recursively compresses files in the directories

-1 thru 9	Specifies the compression level on a scale of 1 thru 9

gzip more or less works on a file-by-file basis and not on an archive basis like some Windows O/S zip utilities. The main reason for this is that tar already provides advanced archiving features. gzip is designed to provide only a compression mechanism.

Hence, when thinking of gzip, think of a single file. When thinking of multiple files, think of tar archives. Let's now explore this with our previous tar archive.

Note – Seasoned Linux professionals will often refer to a tarred archive as a tarball.

Let's make another tar archive from our rsync backup.

```
[root@centos Documents]# tar -cvf RemoteStuff.tar ./RemoteStuff/
[root@centos Documents]# ls
RemoteStuff.tar RemoteStuff/
```

For demonstration purposes, let's gzip the newly created tarball, and tell gzip to keep the old file. By default, without the -c option, gzip will replace the entire tar archive with a .gz file.

```
[root@centos Documents]# gzip -c RemoteStuff.tar > RemoteStuff.tar.gz
[root@centos Documents]# ls
RemoteStuff RemoteStuff.tar RemoteStuff.tar.gz
We now have our original directory, our tarred directory and finally our gziped tarball.
```

Let's try to test the -l switch with gzip.

```
[root@centos Documents]# gzip -l RemoteStuff.tar.gz
    compressed      uncompressed      ratio uncompressed_name
    2317140467      2326661120        0.4% RemoteStuff.tar

[root@centos Documents]#
```

To demonstrate how gzip differs from Windows Zip Utilities, let's run gzip on a folder of text files.

```
[root@centos Documents]# ls text_files/
file1.txt file2.txt file3.txt file4.txt file5.txt
[root@centos Documents]#
```

Now let's use the -r option to recursively compress all the text files in the directory.

```
[root@centos Documents]# gzip -9 -r text_files/
[root@centos Documents]# ls ./text_files/
file1.txt.gz file2.txt.gz file3.txt.gz file4.txt.gz file5.txt.gz
[root@centos Documents]#
```

See? Not what some may have anticipated. All the original text files were removed and each was compressed individually. Because of this behavior, it is best to think of gzip alone when needing to work in single files.

Working with tarballs, let's extract our rsynced tarball into a new directory.

```
[root@centos Documents]# tar -C /tmp -zxvf RemoteStuff.tar.gz
./RemoteStuff/
```

```
./RemoteStuff/.DS_Store
./RemoteStuff/DDWRT/
./RemoteStuff/DDWRT/.DS_Store
./RemoteStuff/DDWRT/ddwrt-linksys-wrt1200acv2-webflash.bin
./RemoteStuff/DDWRT/ddwrt_mod_notes.docx
./RemoteStuff/DDWRT/factory-to-ddwrt.bin
./RemoteStuff/open_ldap_config_notes/
./RemoteStuff/open_ldap_config_notes/ldap_directory_a.png
./RemoteStuff/open_ldap_config_notes/open_ldap_notes.txt
./RemoteStuff/perl_scripts/
./RemoteStuff/perl_scripts/mysnmp.pl
./RemoteStuff/php_scripts/
./RemoteStuff/php_scripts/chunked.php
```

As seen above, we extracted and decompressed our tarball into the /tmp directory.

```
[root@centos Documents]# ls /tmp
hsperfdata_root
RemoteStuff
```

Encrypt TarBall Archives

Encrypting tarball archives for storing secure documents that may need to be accessed by other employees of the organization, in case of disaster recovery, can be a tricky concept. There are basically three ways to do this: either use GnuPG, or use openssl, or use a third part utility.

GnuPG is primarily designed for asymmetric encryption and has an identity-association in mind rather than a passphrase. True, it can be used with symmetrical encryption, but this is not the main strength of GnuPG. Thus, I would discount GnuPG for storing archives with physical security when more people than the original person may need access (like maybe a corporate manager who wants to protect against an Administrator holding all the keys to the kingdom as leverage).

Openssl like GnuPG can do what we want and ships with CentOS. But again, is not specifically designed to do what we want and encryption has been questioned in the security community.

Our choice is a utility called 7zip. 7zip is a compression utility like gzip but with many more features. Like Gnu Gzip, 7zip and its standards are in the open-source community. We just need to install 7zip from our EHEL Repository (the next chapter will cover installing the Extended Enterprise Repositories in detail).

Install 7zip on Centos

7zip is a simple install once our EHEL repositories have been loaded and configured in CentOS.

```
[root@centos Documents]# yum -y install p7zip.x86_64 p7zip-plugins.x86_64
Loaded plugins: fastestmirror, langpacks
base
| 3.6 kB  00:00:00
epel/x86_64/metalink
```

```
|  13 kB  00:00:00
epel
|  4.3 kB  00:00:00
extras
|  3.4 kB  00:00:00
updates
|  3.4 kB  00:00:00
(1/2): epel/x86_64/updateinfo
|  756 kB  00:00:04
(2/2):
epel/x86_64/primary_db
|  4.6 MB  00:00:18
Loading mirror speeds from cached hostfile
--> Running transaction check
---> Package p7zip.x86_64 0:16.02-2.el7 will be installed
---> Package p7zip-plugins.x86_64 0:16.02-2.el7 will be installed
--> Finished Dependency Resolution
Dependencies Resolved
```

Simple as that, 7zip is installed and ready be used with 256-bit AES encryption for our tarball archives.

Now let's use 7z to encrypt our gzipped archive with a password. The syntax for doing so is pretty simple −

```
7z a -p <output filename><input filename>
```

Where, a: add to archive, and -p: encrypt and prompt for passphrase

```
[root@centos Documents]# 7z a -p RemoteStuff.tgz.7z RemoteStuff.tar.gz
7-Zip [64] 16.02 : Copyright (c) 1999-2016 Igor Pavlov : 2016-05-21
p7zip Version 16.02 (locale=en_US.UTF-8,Utf16=on,HugeFiles=on,64 bits,1 CPU Intel(R)
Core(TM) i5-4278U CPU @ 2.60GHz (40651),ASM,AES-NI)
Scanning the drive:
1 file, 2317140467 bytes (2210 MiB)
Creating archive: RemoteStuff.tgz.7z
Items to compress: 1
Enter password (will not be echoed):
Verify password (will not be echoed) :
Files read from disk: 1
Archive size: 2280453410 bytes (2175 MiB)
Everything is Ok
[root@centos Documents]# ls
RemoteStuff RemoteStuff.tar RemoteStuff.tar.gz RemoteStuff.tgz.7z slapD
text_files
[root@centos Documents]#
```

Now, we have our .7z archive that encrypts the gzipped tarball with 256-bit AES.

Note − 7zip uses AES 256-bit encryption with an SHA-256 hash of the password and counter, repeated up to 512K times for key derivation. This should be secure enough if a complex key is used.

The process of encrypting and recompressing the archive further can take some time with larger archives.

7zip is an advanced offering with more features than gzip or bzip2. However, it is not as standard with CentOS or amongst the Linux world. Thus, the other utilities should be used often as possible.

LINUX ADMIN - SYSTEM UPDATES

The CentOS 7 system can be updated in three ways −

❖ Manually
❖ Automatically
❖ Update manually for major security issues and configure automatic updates

In a production environment, it is recommended to update manually for production servers. Or at least establish an update plan so the administrator can assure services vital to business operations.

It is plausible a simple security update can cause recursive issues with common application that requires upgrading and reconfiguration by an Administrator. So, be weary of scheduling automatic updates in production before testing in development servers and desktops first.

Manually Update CentOS 7

To update CentOS 7, we will want to become familiar with the yum command. yum is used to deal with package repositories in CentOS 7. yum is the tool commonly used to −

❖ Update the CentOS 7 Linux System
❖ Search for packages
❖ Install packages
❖ Detect and install required dependencies for packages

In order to use yum for updates, your CentOS server will need to be connected to the Internet. Most configurations will install a base system, then use yum to query the main CentOS repository for additional functionality in packages and apply system updates.

We have already made use of yum to install a few packages. When using yum you will always need to do so as the root user. Or a user with root access. So let's search for and install an easy to use text-editor called nano.

```
[root@centos rdc]# yum search nano
Loaded plugins: fastestmirror, langpacks
Loading mirror speeds from cached hostfile
 * base: mirror.rackspace.com
 * epel: mirror.chpc.utah.edu
 * extras: repos.forethought.net
 * updates: repos.forethought.net
===============================================================================
=
    N/S matched: nano
===============================================================================
=
nano.x86_64 : A small text editor
nodejs-nano.noarch : Minimalistic couchdb driver for Node.js
perl-Time-Clock.noarch : Twenty-four hour clock object with nanosecond precision
  Name and summary matches only, use "search all" for everything.
```

```
[root@centos rdc]#
```

Now, let's install the nano text editor.

```
[root@centos rdc]# yum install nano
Loaded plugins: fastestmirror, langpacks
Loading mirror speeds from cached hostfile
* base: mirror.keystealth.org
* epel: pubmirror1.math.uh.edu
* extras: centos.den.host-engine.com
* updates: repos.forethought.net
Resolving Dependencies
--> Running transaction check
---> Package nano.x86_64 0:2.3.1-10.el7 will be installed
--> Finished Dependency Resolution
Dependencies Resolved
=================================================================
===========
Package          Arch
Version          Repository          Size
=================================================================
===========
Installing:
nano             x86_64
2.3.1-10.el7     base                440 k

Transaction Summary
Install  1 Package
Total download size: 440 k
Installed size: 1.6 M
Is this ok [y/d/N]: y
Downloading packages:
nano-2.3.1-10.el7.x86_64.rpm
| 440 kB  00:00:00
Running transaction check
Running transaction test
Transaction test succeeded
Running transaction
 Installing : nano-2.3.1-10.el7.x86_64
1/1
 Verifying  : nano-2.3.1-10.el7.x86_64
1/1
Installed:
 nano.x86_64 0:2.3.1-10.el7

Complete!
[root@centos rdc]#
```

We have installed the nano text editor. This method, IMO, is a lot easier than searching for utilities on websites and manually running the installers. Also, repositories use digital signatures to validate packages assuring they are coming from a trusted source with yum. It is up to the administrator to validate authenticity when trusting new repositories. This is why it is considered a best practice to be weary of third party repositories.

Yum can also be used to remove a package.

```
[root@centos rdc]# yum remove nano
Loaded plugins: fastestmirror, langpacks
Resolving Dependencies
--> Running transaction check
---> Package nano.x86_64 0:2.3.1-10.el7 will be erased
--> Finished Dependency Resolution
Dependencies Resolved
```

Now let's check for updates.

```
[root@centos rdc]# yum list updates
Loaded plugins: fastestmirror, langpacks
Loading mirror speeds from cached hostfile
 * base: mirror.keystealth.org
 * epel: pubmirror1.math.uh.edu
 * extras: centos.den.host-engine.com
 * updates: repos.forethought.net
Updated Packages
NetworkManager.x86_64          1:1.4.0-17.el7_3     updates
NetworkManager-adsl.x86_64     1:1.4.0-17.el7_3     updates
NetworkManager-glib.x86_64     1:1.4.0-17.el7_3     updates
NetworkManager-libnm.x86_64    1:1.4.0-17.el7_3     updates
NetworkManager-team.x86_64     1:1.4.0-17.el7_3     updates
NetworkManager-tui.x86_64      1:1.4.0-17.el7_3     updates
NetworkManager-wifi.x86_64     1:1.4.0-17.el7_3     updates
audit.x86_64                   2.6.5-3.el7_3.1      updates
audit-libs.x86_64              2.6.5-3.el7_3.1      updates
audit-libs-python.x86_64
```

As depicted, we have a few dozen updates pending to install. Actually, there are about 100 total updates since we have not yet configured automatic updates. Thus, let's install all pending updates.

```
[root@centos rdc]# yum update
Loaded plugins: fastestmirror, langpacks
Loading mirror speeds from cached hostfile
 * base: mirrors.usc.edu
 * epel: pubmirror1.math.uh.edu
 * extras: repos.forethought.net
 * updates: repos.forethought.net
Resolving Dependencies
--> Running transaction check
---> Package NetworkManager.x86_64 1:1.4.0-14.el7_3 will be updated
---> Package NetworkManager.x86_64 1:1.4.0-17.el7_3 will be an update
selinux-policy            noarch    3.13.1102.el7_3.15    updates    414 k
selinux-policy-targeted   noarch    3.13.1102.el7_3.15    updates    6.4 M
systemd                   x86_64    21930.el7_3.7         updates    5.2 M
systemd-libs              x86_64    21930.el7_3.7         updates    369 k
systemd-python            x86_64    21930.el7_3.7         updates    109 k
systemd-sysv              x86_64    21930.el7_3.7         updates    63 k
tcsh                      x86_64    6.18.01-13.el7_3.1    updates    338 k
tzdata                    noarch    2017a1.el7            updates    443 k
tzdata-java               noarch    2017a1.el7            updates    182 k
wpa_supplicant            x86_64    1:2.021.el7_3         updates    788 k
Transaction Summary
================================================================================
==========
Install  2 Packages
Upgrade  68 Packages
Total size: 196 M
Total download size: 83 M
Is this ok [y/d/N]:
```

After hitting the "y" key, updating of CentOS 7 will commence. The general process that yum goes through when updating is –

- ❖ Checks the current packages
- ❖ Looks in the repository for updated packages
- ❖ Calculates dependencies needed for updated packages
- ❖ Downloads updates

❖   Installs updates

Now, let's make sure our system is up to date −

```
[root@centos rdc]# yum list updates
Loaded plugins: fastestmirror, langpacks
Loading mirror speeds from cached hostfile
 * updates: mirror.compevo.com
[root@centos rdc]#
```

As you can see, there are no updates listed.

Configure Automatic Updates for YUM

In an Enterprise environment, as mentioned earlier, automatic updates may or may not be the preferred method of installation. Let's go over the steps for configuring automatic updates with yum.

First, we install a package called yum-cron.

```
[root@centos rdc]# yum -y install yum-cron
Install 1 Package
Total download size: 61 k
Installed size: 51 k
Downloading packages:
yum-cron-3.4.3-150.el7.centos.noarch.rpm
 | 61 kB  00:00:01
Running transaction check
Running transaction test
Transaction test succeeded
Running transaction
 Installing : yum-cron-3.4.3-150.el7.centos.noarch
1/1
 Verifying  : yum-cron-3.4.3-150.el7.centos.noarch
1/1
Installed:
 yum-cron.noarch 0:3.4.3-150.el7.centos

Complete!
[root@centos rdc]#
```

By default, yum-cron will only download updates and not install them. Whether to install updates automatically is on the Administrator. The biggest caveat is: some updates will require a system reboot. Also, some updates may require a configuration change before services are again operational.

Updating dependencies can possibly create a recursive problem in the following situation −

❖   An update is recommended by yum for a certain library
❖   The library only supports Apache Server 2.4, but we have server 2.3
❖   Our commerce site relies on a certain version of PHP
❖   The new version of Apache installed for the library requires upgrading PHP
❖   Our production web applications have not yet been tested with the newer PHP version

Yum may go ahead and automatically upgrade Apache and PHP without notice unless configured not to.

If all 5 scenarios play out, it can result in anything from a big headache in the morning to a possible security compromise exposing the user data. While the aforementioned example is a perfect storm of sorts, we never want such a scenario to play out.

It is up to the Administrator for accessing possible scenarios of potential revenue loss from time needed to restore services due to possible downtime from update reboots and reconfigurations. This practice may not be conservative enough for, say, a multi-million dollar per day ecommerce site with millions of customers.

Now let's configure yum-cron to automatically install system updates.

```
[root@centos rdc]# vim /etc/yum/yum-cron.conf
# Whether updates should be applied when they are available.  Note
# that download_updates must also be yes for the update to be applied.
apply_updates = yes
```

We want to change apply_updates = no to apply_updates = yes. Now let's configure the update interval for yum-cron.

Again, whether to use automatic updates and install updates on demand can be a double edged sword and needs to be considered by an administrator for each unique situation.

LINUX ADMIN - SHELL SCRIPTING

Introduction to Bash Shell

Like flavors of GNU Linux, shells come in many varieties and vary in compatibility. The default shell in CentOS is known as the Bash or Bourne Again Shell. The Bash shell is a modern day, modified version of Bourne Shell developed by Stephen Bourne. Bash was the direct replacement to the original Thompson Shell on the Unix operating system developed at Bell Labs by Ken Thompson and Dennis Ritchie (Stephen Bourne was also employed by Bell Labs)

Everyone has a favorite shell and each has its strengths and difficulties. But for the most part, Bash is going to be the default shell across all Linux distributions and most commonly available. With experience, everyone will want to explore and use a shell that is best for them. However at the same time, everyone will also want to master Bash shell.

Other Linux shells include: Tcsh, Csh, Ksh, Zsh, and Fish.

Developing skills to use any Linux shell at an expert level is extremely important to a CentOS administrator. As we mentioned previously, unlike Windows, Linux at its heart is a command line operating system. A shell is simply a user interface that allows an administrator (or user) to issue commands to the operating system. If a Linux system administrator were an airlines pilot, using the shell would be similar to taking the plane off auto-pilot and grabbing the manual controls for more maneuverable flight.

A Linux shell, like Bash, is known in Computer Science terms as a Command Line Interpreter. Microsoft Windows also has two command line interpreters called DOS (not to be confused with the original DOS operating system) and PowerShell.

Most modern shells like Bash provide constructs allowing more complex shell scripts to automate both common and complex tasks.

Constructs include −

- ❖ Script flow control (ifthen and else)
- ❖ Logical comparison operations (greater than, less than, equality)
- ❖ Loops
- ❖ Variables
- ❖ Parameters defining operation (similar to switches with commands)

Using Shell Script Versus Scripting Language

Often when thinking about performing a task administrators ask themselves: Should I use a shell script or a scripting language such as Perl, Ruby or Python?

There is no set rule here. There are only typical differences between shells versus scripting languages.

Shell

Shell allows the use of Linux commands such as sed, grep, tee, cat and all other command-line based utilities on the Linux operating system. In fact, pretty much any command line Linux utility can be scripted in your shell.

A great example of using a shell would be a quick script to check a list of hosts for DNS resolution.

Our simple Bash Script to check DNS names −

```
#!/bin/bash
for name in $(cat $1);
  do
    host $name.$2 | grep "has address"
  done
exit
```

small wordlist to test DNS resolution on −

```
dns
www
test
dev
mail
rdp
remote
```

Output against google.com domain −

```
[rdc@centos ~]$ ./dns-check.sh dns-names.txt google.com
-doing dns
dns.google.com has address 172.217.6.46
-doing www
www.google.com has address 172.217.6.36
-doing test
-doing dev
-doing mail
googlemail.l.google.com has address 172.217.6.37
-doing rdp
-doing remote
[rdc@centos ~]$
```

Leveraging simple Linux commands in our shell, we were able to make a simple 5-line script to audit DNS names from a word list. This would have taken some considerable time in Perl, Python, or Ruby even when using a nicely implemented DNS Library.

Scripting Language

A scripting language will give more control outside the shell. The above Bash script used a wrapper around the Linux host command. What if we wanted to do more and make our own application like host to interact outside the shell? This is where we would use a scripting language.

Also, with a highly maintained scripting language we know our actions will work across different systems for the most part. Python 3.5, for example, will work on any other system running Python 3.5 with the same libraries installed. Not so, if we want to run our BASH script on both Linux and HP-UX.

Sometimes the lines between a scripting language and a powerful shell can be blurred. It is possible to automate CentOS Linux administration tasks with Python, Perl or Ruby. Doing so is really quite commonplace. Also, affluent shell-script developers have made a simple, but otherwise functional, web-server daemon in Bash.

With experience in scripting languages and automating tasks in shells, a CentOS administrator will be able to quickly determine where to start when needing to solve a problem. It is quite common to start a project with a shell script. Then progress to a scripting (or compiled) language as a project gets more complex.

Also, it is ok to use both a scripting language and shell script for different parts of a project. An example could be a Perl script to scrape a website. Then, use a shell script to parse and format with sed, awk, and egrep. Finally, use a PHP script for inserting formatted data into MySQL database using a web GUI.

With some theory behind shells, let's get started with the basic building blocks to automate tasks from a Bash shell in CentOS.

Input Output and Redirection

Processing stdout to another command −

```
[rdc@centos ~]$ cat ~/output.txt | wc -l
6039
```

Above, we have passed cat'sstoud to wc for processing with the pipe character. wc then processed the output from cat, printing the line count of output.txt to the terminal. Think of the pipe character as a "pipe" passing output from one command, to be processed by the next command.

Following are the key concepts to remember when dealing with command redirection −

Number	File descriptor	Character
0	standard input	<
1	standard output	>
2	standard error	
	append stdout	>>
	assign redirection	&
	pipe stdout into stdin		

We introduced this in chapter one without really talking much about redirection or assigning redirection. When opening a terminal in Linux, your shell is seen as the default target for −

- ❖ standard input < 0
- ❖ standard output > 1
- ❖ standard error 2

Let's see how this works –

```
[rdc@centos ~]$ lsof -ap $BASHPID -d 0,1,2
COMMAND  PID   USER  **FD**  TYPE DEVICE  SIZE/OFF NODE   NAME
bash     13684 rdc   **0u**  CHR  136,0   0t0   3   /dev/pts/0
bash     13684 rdc   **1u**  CHR  136,0   0t0   3   /dev/pts/0
bash     13684 rdc   **2u**  CHR  136,0   0t0   3   /dev/pts/0
[rdc@centos ~]$
```

/dev/pts/0 is our pseudo terminal. CentOS Linux looks at this and thinks of our open terminal application like a real terminal with the keyboard and display plugged in through a serial interface. However, like a hypervisor abstracts hardware to an operating system /dev/pts abstracts our terminal to applications.

From the above lsof command, we can see under the FD column that all three file-descriptors are set to our virtual terminal (0,1,2). We can now send commands, see command output, as well as any errors associated with the command.

Following are examples for STDIN and STDOUT –

STDOUT

```
[root@centosLocal centos]# echo "I am coming from Standard output or STDOUT." >
output.txt && cat output.txt
I am coming from Standard output or STDOUT.
[root@centosLocal centos]#
```

It is also possible to send both stdout and stderr to separate files –

```
bash-3.2# find / -name passwd 1> good.txt 2> err.txt
bash-3.2# cat good.txt
/etc/pam.d/passwd
/etc/passwd
bash-3.2# cat err.txt
find: /dev/fd/3: Not a directory
find: /dev/fd/4: Not a directory
bash-3.2#
```

When searching the entire file system, two errors were encountered. Each were sent to a separate file for later perusal, while the results returned were placed into a separate text file.

Sending stderr to a text file can be useful when doing things that output a lot of data to the terminal like compiling applications. This will allow for perusal of errors that could get lost from terminal scrollback history.

One note when passing STDOUT to a text file are the differences between >> and >. The double ">>" will append to a file, while the singular form will clobber the file and write new contents (so all previous data will be lost).

STDIN

```
[root@centosLocal centos]# cat < stdin.txt
Hello,
I am being read form Standard input, STDIN.
[root@centosLocal centos]#
```

In the above command, the text file stdin.txt was redirected to the cat command which echoed its content to STDOUT.

The pipe character " | "

The pipe character will take the output from the first command, passing it as an input into the next command, allowing the secondary command to perform operations on the output.

Now, let's "pipe" the stdout of cat to another command −

```
[root@centosLocal centos]# cat output.txt | wc -l
2
[root@centosLocal centos]#
```

Above, wc performs calculations on output from cat which was passed from the pipe. The pipe command is particularly useful when filtering the output from grep or egrep −

```
[root@centosLocal centos]# egrep "^[0-9]{4}$" /usr/dicts/nums | wc -l
9000
[root@centosLocal centos]#
```

In the above command, we passed every 4 digit number to wc from a text file containing all numbers from 65535 passed through an egrep filter.

Redirecting Output with &

Output can be redirected using the & character. If we want to direct the output both STDOUT and STDERR, into the same file, it can be accomplished as follows −

```
[root@centosLocal centos]# find / -name passwd > out.txt 2>&1
[root@centosLocal centos]# cat out.txt
find: /dev/fd/3: Not a directory
find: /dev/fd/4: Not a directory
/etc/passwd
[root@centosLocal centos]#
```

Redirecting using the & character works like this: first, the output is redirected into out.txt. Second, STDERR or the file descriptor 2 is reassigned to the same location as STDOUT, in this case out.txt.

Redirection is extremely useful and comes in handy while solving problems that surgace when manipulating large text-files, compiling source code, redirecting the output in shell scripts, and issuing complex Linux commands.

While powerful, redirection can get complicated for newer CentOS Administrators. Practice, research, and occasional question to a Linux forum (such as Stack Overflow Linux) will help solve advanced solutions.

Bash Shell Constructs

Now that we have a good idea of how the Bash shell works, let's learn some basic constructs, commonly used, to write scripts. In this section we will explore −

- ❖ Variables
- ❖ Loops
- ❖ Conditionals
- ❖ Loop control
- ❖ Reading and writing to files
- ❖ Basic math operations

BASH Troubleshooting Hints

BASH can be a little tricky compared to a dedicated scripting language. Some of the biggest hang-ups in BASH scripts are from incorrectly escaping or not escaping script operations being passed to the shell. If you have looked over a script a few times and it is not working as expected, don't fret. This is common even with those who use BASH to create complex scripts daily.

A quick search of Google or signing up at an expert Linux forum to ask a question will lead to a quick resolution. There is a very likely chance someone has come across the exact issue and it has already been solved.

BASH scripting is a great method of quickly creating powerful scripts for everything from automating administration tasks to creating useful tools. Becoming an expert level BASH script developer takes time and practice. Hence, use BASH scripts whenever possible, it is a great tool to have in your CentOS Administration toolbox.

LINUX ADMIN - PACKAGE MANAGEMENT

Package management in CentOS can be performed in two ways: from the terminal and from the Graphical User Interface.

More often than not a majority of a CentOS administrator's time will be using the terminal. Updating and installing packages for CentOS is no different. With this in mind, we will first explore package management in the terminal, then touch on using the graphical package management tool provided by CentOS.

YUM Package Manager

YUM is the tool provided for package management in CentOS. We have briefly touched this topic in previous chapters. In this chapter, we will be working from a clean CentOS install. We will first completely update our installation and then install an application.

YUM has brought software installation and management in Linux a long way. YUM "automagically" checks for out-of-date dependencies, in addition to out-of-date packages. This has really taken a load off the CentOS administrator compared to the old days of compiling every application from source-code.

yum check-update

Checks for packages that can update candidates. For this tutorial, we will assume this a production system that will be facing the Internet with no production applications that needs to be tested by DevOps before upgrading the packages. Let us now install the updated candidates onto the system.

```
[root@localhost rdc]# yum check-update
Loaded plugins: fastestmirror, langpacks
Loading mirror speeds from cached hostfile
 * base: mirror.scalabledns.com
 * extras: mirror.scalabledns.com
 * updates: mirror.clarkson.edu
NetworkManager.x86_64              1:1.4.0-19.el7_3          updates
NetworkManager-adsl.x86_64           1:1.4.0-19.el7_3          updates
NetworkManager-glib.x86_64           1:1.4.0-19.el7_3          updates
NetworkManager-libnm.x86_64            1:1.4.0-19.el7_3          updates
NetworkManager-team.x86_64           1:1.4.0-19.el7_3          updates
NetworkManager-tui.x86_64            1:1.4.0-19.el7_3          updates
NetworkManager-wifi.x86_64           1:1.4.0-19.el7_3          updates
audit.x86_64              2.6.5-3.el7_3.1        updates
vim-common.x86_64            2:7.4.160-1.el7_3.1        updates
vim-enhanced.x86_64           2:7.4.160-1.el7_3.1        updates
vim-filesystem.x86_64          2:7.4.160-1.el7_3.1        updates
vim-minimal.x86_64           2:7.4.160-1.el7_3.1        updates
wpa_supplicant.x86_64           1:2.0-21.el7_3          updates
xfsprogs.x86_64             4.5.0-9.el7_3          updates
[root@localhost rdc]#
```

yum update

This will install all updated candidates making your CentOS installation current. With a new installation, this can take a little time depending on your installation and your internet connection speed.

```
[root@localhost rdc]# yum update
vim-minimal            x86_64   2:7.4.160-1.el7_3.1   updates   436 k
wpa_supplicant         x86_64   1:2.0-21.el7_3        updates   788 k
xfsprogs               x86_64   4.5.0-9.el7_3         updates   895 k
Transaction Summary
=============================================================================
==================
Install   2 Packages
Upgrade  156 Packages
Total download size: 371 M
Is this ok [y/d/N]:
```

Install Software via YUM

Besides updating the CentOS system, the YUM package manager is our go-to tool for installing the software. Everything from network monitoring tools, video players, to text editors can be installed from a central repository with YUM.

Before installing some software utilities, let's look at few YUM commands. For daily work, 90% of a CentOS Admin's usage of YUM will be with about 7 commands. We will go over each in the hope of becoming familiar with operating YUM at a proficient level for daily use. However, like most Linux utilities, YUM offers a wealth of advanced features that are always great to explore via the man page. Use man yum will always be the first step to performing unfamiliar operations with any Linux utility.

Most Common YUM Commands

Following are the commonly used YUM commands.

Command	Action
list installed	Lists packages installed via YUM
list all	Lists all currently available packages
group list	Lists grouped packages
info	Provides detailed information about a package
search	Searches package descriptions and names
install	Installs a package
localinstall	Installs a local rpm package
remove	Removes and installs package
clean all	Cleans /var/cache/yum to free disk-space
man yum	Like all linux commands, the help file

Install Software with YUM

We will now install a text-based web browser called Lynx. Before installation, we must first get the package name containing the Lynx web browser. We are not even 100% sure our default CentOS repository provides a package for the Lynx web browser, so let's search and see −

```
[root@localhost rdc]# yum search web browser
Loaded plugins: fastestmirror, langpacks
Loading mirror speeds from cached hostfile
 * base: mirror.scalabledns.com
 * extras: mirror.scalabledns.com
 * updates: mirror.clarkson.edu
================================================================
N/S matched: web, browser
================================================================
icedtea-web.x86_64 : Additional Java components for OpenJDK - Java browser
plug-in and Web Start implementation
elinks.x86_64 : A text-mode Web browser
firefox.i686 : Mozilla Firefox Web browser
firefox.x86_64 : Mozilla Firefox Web browser
lynx.x86_64 : A text-based Web browser
Full name and summary matches only, use "search all" for everything.

[root@localhost rdc]#
```

We see, CentOS does offer the Lynx web browser in the repository. Let's see some more information about the package.

```
[root@localhost rdc]# lynx.x86_64
bash: lynx.x86_64: command not found...
[root@localhost rdc]# yum info lynx.x86_64
Loaded plugins: fastestmirror, langpacks
Loading mirror speeds from cached hostfile
 * base: mirror.scalabledns.com
 * extras: mirror.scalabledns.com
 * updates: mirror.clarkson.edu
Available Packages
Name      : lynx
Arch      : x86_64
Version   : 2.8.8
Release   : 0.3.dev15.el7
Size      : 1.4 M
Repo      : base/7/x86_64
Summary   : A text-based Web browser
URL       : http://lynx.isc.org/
License   : GPLv2
Description : Lynx is a text-based Web browser. Lynx does not display any images,
          : but it does support frames, tables, and most other HTML tags. One
          : advantage Lynx has over graphical browsers is speed; Lynx starts and
          : exits quickly and swiftly displays web pages.

[root@localhost rdc]#
```

Nice! Version 2.8 is current enough so let's install Lynx.

```
[root@localhost rdc]# yum install lynx
Loaded plugins: fastestmirror, langpacks
Loading mirror speeds from cached hostfile
 * base: mirror.scalabledns.com
 * extras: mirror.scalabledns.com
 * updates: mirror.clarkson.edu
Resolving Dependencies
--> Running transaction check
---> Package lynx.x86_64 0:2.8.8-0.3.dev15.el7 will be installed
--> Finished Dependency Resolution
Dependencies Resolved
================================================================
==========
```

```
====================================================================
============
Package              Arch
Version            Repository          Size
====================================================================
============
====================================================================
============
Installing:
lynx                  x86_64
2.8.80.3.dev15.el7    base                1.4 M
Transaction Summary
====================================================================
============
====================================================================
============
Install  1 Package
Total download size: 1.4 M
Installed size: 5.4 M
Is this ok [y/d/N]: y
Downloading packages:
No Presto metadata available for base
lynx-2.8.8-0.3.dev15.el7.x86_64.rpm
| 1.4 MB  00:00:10
Running transaction check
Running transaction test
Transaction test succeeded
Running transaction
  Installing : lynx-2.8.8-0.3.dev15.el7.x86_64
1/1
  Verifying  : lynx-2.8.8-0.3.dev15.el7.x86_64
1/1
Installed:
  lynx.x86_64 0:2.8.8-0.3.dev15.el7
Complete!
[root@localhost rdc]#
```

Next, let's make sure Lynx did in fact install correctly.

```
[root@localhost rdc]# yum list installed | grep -i lynx
lynx.x86_64            2.8.8-0.3.dev15.el7         @base
[root@localhost rdc]#
```

Great! Let's use Lynx to and see what the web looks like without "likes" and pretty pictures.

```
[root@localhost rdc]# lynx www.tutorialpoint.in
```

Great, now we have a web browser for our production server that can be used without much worry into remote exploits launched over the web. This a good thing for production servers.

We are almost completed, however first we need to set this server for developers to test applications. Thus, let's make sure they have all the tools needed for their job. We could install everything individually, but CentOS and YUM have made this a lot faster. Let's install the Development Group Package.

```
[root@localhost rdc]# yum groups list
Loaded plugins: fastestmirror, langpacks
Loading mirror speeds from cached hostfile
 * base: mirror.scalabledns.com
 * extras: mirror.scalabledns.com
 * updates: mirror.clarkson.edu

Available Groups:
   Compatibility Libraries
   Console Internet Tools
   Development Tools
   Graphical Administration Tools
   Legacy UNIX Compatibility
   Scientific Support
   Security Tools
   Smart Card Support
   System Administration Tools
   System Management
Done
[root@localhost rdc]#
```

This is a smaller list of Package Groups provided by CentOS. Let's see what is included with the "Development Group".

```
[root@localhost rdc]# yum group info "Development Tools"
Loaded plugins: fastestmirror, langpacks
```

```
There is no installed groups file.
Maybe run: yum groups mark convert (see man yum)
Loading mirror speeds from cached hostfile
 * base: mirror.scalabledns.com
 * extras: mirror.scalabledns.com
 * updates: mirror.clarkson.edu

Group: Development Tools
Group-Id: development
Description: A basic development environment.
Mandatory Packages:
autoconf
automake
binutils
bison
```

The first screen of output is as seen above. This entire list is rather comprehensive. However, this group will usually be needed to be installed in its entirety as time goes by. Let's install the entire Development Group.

```
[root@localhost rdc]# yum groupinstall "Development Tools"
```

This will be a larger install. When completed, your server will have most development libraries and compilers for Perl, Python, C, and C++.

Graphical Package Management in CentOS

Gnome Desktop provides a graphical package management tool called Software. It is fairly simple to use and straightforward. Software, the Gnome package management tool for CentOS can be found by navigating to: Applications → System Tools → Software.

The Software Package Management Tool is divided into groups allowing the administrator to select packages for installation. While this tool is great for ease-of-use and simplicity for end-users, YUM is a lot more powerful and will probably be used more by administrators.

Following is a screenshot of the Software Package Management Tool, not really designed for System Administrators.

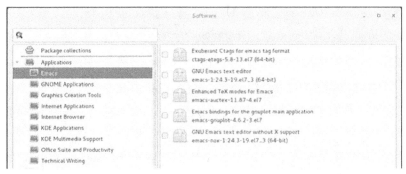

LINUX ADMIN - VOLUME MANAGEMENT

Logical Volume Management (LVM) is a method used by Linux to manage storage volumes across different physical hard disks. This is not to be confused with RAID. However, it can be thought of in a similar concept as RAID 0 or J-Bod. With LVM, it is possible to have (for example) three physical disks of 1TB each, then a logical volume of around 3TB such as /dev/sdb. Or even two logical volumes of 1.5TB, 5 volumes of 500GB, or any combination. One single disk can even be used for snapshots of Logical Volumes.

Note – Using Logical Volumes actually increases disk I/O when configured correctly. This works in a similar fashion to RAID 0 striping data across separate disks.

When learning about volume management with LVM, it is easier if we know what each component in LVM is. Please study the following table to get a firm grasp of each component. If you need to, use Google to study. Understanding each piece of a logical volume is important to manage them.

PV	Physical Volume	sda
PP	Physical Partition	sda1 , sda2
VG	Volume Group	Pooled physical resources
LV	Logical Volume	Seen as a storage facility to the operating system

A physical volume will be seen as /dev/sda, /dev/sdb; a physical disk that is detected by Linux.

A physical partition will be a section of the disk partitioned by a disk utility such as fdisk. Keep in mind, physical partition is not recommended in most common LVM setups. Example: disk /dev/sda is partitioned to include two physical partitions: /dev/sda1 and /dev/sda1

If we have two physical disks of 1TB each, we can create a volume group of almost 2TB amongst the two.

From the volume group, we can create three logical volumes each of any-size not exceeding the total volume group size.

Traditional Linux Disk Administration Tools

Before being acquainted with the latest and greatest featured tools for LVM Management in CentOS 7, we should first explore more traditional tools that have been used for Linux disk management. These tools will come handy and still have use with today's advanced LVM tools such as the System Storage Manager: lsblk, parted, and mkfs.xfs.

Now, assuming we have added another disk or two to our system, we need to enumerate disks detected by Linux. I'd always advise enumerating disks every time before performing operations considered as destructive. lsblk is a great tool for getting disk information. Let's see what disks CentOS detects.

```
[root@localhost rdc]# lsblk
NAME       MAJ:MIN  RM  SIZE  RO  TYPE MOUNTPOINT
sda         8:0    0   20G   0    disk
├─sda1      8:1    0   1G    0    part /boot
└─sda2      8:2    0   19G   0    part
  ├─cl-root 253:0  0   17G   0    lvm  /
  └─cl-swap 253:1  0   2G    0    lvm  [SWAP]
sdb         8:16   0   6G    0    disk
sdc         8:32   0   4G    0    disk
sr0        11:0    1  1024M  0    rom
```

As you can see, we have three disks on this system: sda, sdb, and sdc.

Disk sda contains our working CentOS installation, so we do not want to toy around with sda. Both sdb and sdc were added to the system for this tutorial. Let's make these disks usable to CentOS.

Create a Disk Label

```
[root@localhost rdc]# parted /dev/sdb mklabel GPT
Warning: The existing disk label on /dev/sdb will be destroyed and all data on this
  disk will be lost. Do you want to continue?
Yes/No? Yes
[root@localhost rdc]#
```

We now have one disk labeled. Simply run the parted command in the same manner on sdc.

Create the Partitions on the Disk

We will only create a single partition on each disk. To create partitions, the parted command is used again.

```
[root@localhost rdc]# parted -a opt /dev/sdb mkpart primary ext4 0% 100%
```

Warning – You requested a partition from 0.00B to 6442MB (sectors 0..12582911).

The closest location we can manage is 17.4kB to 1048kB (sectors 34..2047).

Is this still acceptable to you?

Yes/No? NO

```
[root@localhost rdc]# parted -a opt /dev/sdc mkpart primary ext4 0% 100%
```

Information – You may need to update /etc/fstab.

```
[root@localhost rdc]# lsblk
NAME       MAJ:MIN  RM  SIZE  RO  TYPE MOUNTPOINT
sda         8:0    0   20G   0    disk
├─sda1      8:1    0   1G    0    part / boot
└─sda2      8:2    0   19G   0    part
  ├─cl-root 253:0  0   17G   0    lvm  /
  └─cl-swap 253:1  0   2G    0    lvm  [SWAP]
sdb         8:16   0   6G    0    disk
```

```
└─sdb1    8:17   0   6G    0    part
sdc       8:32   0   4G    0    disk
└─sdc1    8:33   0   4G    0    part
sr0       11:0   1  1024M  0    rom
[root@localhost rdc]#
```

As you can see from lsblk output, we now have two partitions, each on sdb and sdc.

Make the File System

Finally, before mounting and using any volume we need to add a file system. We will be using the XFS file system.

```
root@localhost rdc]# mkfs.xfs -f /dev/sdb1
meta-data = /dev/sdb1           isize = 512   agcount = 4, agsize = 393088 blks
         =                      sectsz = 512  attr = 2, projid32bit = 1
         =                      crc = 1    finobt = 0, sparse = 0
data     =                      bsize = 4096   blocks = 1572352, imaxpct = 25
         =                      sunit = 0    swidth = 0 blks
naming   = version 2            bsize = 4096   ascii-ci = 0 ftype = 1
log      = internal log         bsize = 4096   blocks = 2560, version = 2
         =                      sectsz = 512  sunit = 0 blks, lazy-count = 1
realtime = none                 extsz = 4096   blocks = 0, rtextents = 0
[root@localhost rdc]# mkfs.xfs -f /dev/sdc1
meta-data = /dev/sdc1           isize = 512   agcount = 4, agsize = 262016 blks
         =                      sectsz = 512  attr = 2, projid32bit = 1
         =                      crc = 1    finobt = 0, sparse = 0
data     =                      bsize = 4096   blocks = 1048064, imaxpct = 25
         =                      sunit = 0    swidth = 0 blks
naming   = version 2            bsize = 4096   ascii-ci = 0 ftype = 1
log      = internal log         bsize = 4096   blocks = 2560, version = 2
         =                      sectsz = 512  sunit = 0 blks, lazy-count = 1
realtime = none                 extsz = 4096   blocks = 0, rtextents = 0
[root@localhost rdc]#
```

Let's check to make sure each have a usable file system.

```
[root@localhost rdc]# lsblk -o NAME,FSTYPE
NAME         FSTYPE
sda
 ├─sda1      xfs
 └─sda2      LVM2_member
 ├─cl-root   xfs
 └─cl-swap   swap
sdb
 └─sdb1      xfs
sdc
 └─sdc1      xfs
sr0
[root@localhost rdc]#
```

Each is now using the XFS file system. Let's mount them, check the mount, and copy a file to each.

```
[root@localhost rdc]# mount -o defaults /dev/sdb1 /mnt/sdb
[root@localhost rdc]# mount -o defaults /dev/sdc1 /mnt/sdc
[root@localhost ~]# touch /mnt/sdb/myFile /mnt/sdc/myFile
[root@localhost ~]# ls /mnt/sdb /mnt/sdc
/mnt/sdb:
 myFile
/mnt/sdc:
 myFile
```

We have two usable disks at this point. However, they will only be usable when we mount them manually. To mount each on boot, we must edit the fstab file. Also, permissions must be set for groups needing access to the new disks.

Create Volume Groups and Logical Volumes

One of the greatest addition to CentOS 7 was the inclusion of a utility called System Storage Manager or ssm. System Storage Manager greatly simplifies the process of managing LVM pools and storage volumes on Linux.

We will go through the process of creating a simple volume pool and logical volumes in CentOS. The first step is installing the System Storage Manager.

[root@localhost rdc]# yum install system-storage-manager

Let's look at our disks using the ssm list command.

```
[root@localhost rdc]# ssm list
------------------------------------------------------------------------
Device          Free      Used      Total   Pool   Mount point
------------------------------------------------------------------------
/dev/sda                            20.00 GB        PARTITIONED
/dev/sda1                            1.00 GB        /boot
/dev/sda2      0.00 KB  19.00 GB    19.00 GB  cl
/dev/sdb                             6.00 GB
/dev/sdb1                            6.00 GB        /mnt/sdb
/dev/sdc                             4.00 GB
/dev/sdc1                            4.00 GB        /mnt/sdc
------------------------------------------------------------------------

------------------------------------------------------------------------
Pool  Type  Devices    Free      Used      Total
------------------------------------------------------------------------
cl    lvm   1          0.00 KB  19.00 GB  19.00 GB
------------------------------------------------------------------------

------------------------------------------------------------------------
Volume        Pool  Volume size  FS     FS size      Free   Type    Mount point
------------------------------------------------------------------------
/dev/cl/root  cl       17.00 GB  xfs    16.99 GB  13.07 GB  linear  /
/dev/cl/swap  cl        2.00 GB                             linear
/dev/sda1               1.00 GB  xfs   1014.00 MB 786.99 MB  part   /boot
/dev/sdb1               6.00 GB  xfs     5.99 GB   5.99 GB          /mnt/sdb
/dev/sdc1               4.00 GB  xfs     3.99 GB   3.99 GB          /mnt/sdc
------------------------------------------------------------------------
[root@localhost rdc]# ▌
```

As seen above, a total of three disks are installed on the system.

- ❖ /sdba1 – Hosts our CentOS installation
- ❖ /sdb1 – Mounted at /mnt/sdb
- ❖ /sdc1 – Mounted at /mnt/sdc

What we want to do is make a Volume Group using two disks (sdb and sdc). Then make three 3GB Logical Volumes available to the system.

Let's create our Volume Group.

[root@localhost rdc]# ssm create -p NEW_POOL /dev/sdb1 /dev/sdc1

By default, ssm will create a single logical volume extending the entire 10GB of the pool. We don't want this, so let's remove this.

[root@localhost rdc]# ssm remove /dev/NEW_POOL/lvol001
Do you really want to remove active logical volume NEW_POOL/lvol001? [y/n]: y
Logical volume "lvol001" successfully removed
[root@localhost rdc]#

Finally, let's create the three Logical Volumes.

```
[root@localhost rdc]# ssm create -n disk001 --fs xfs -s 3GB -p NEW_POOL
[root@localhost rdc]# ssm create -n disk002 --fs xfs -s 3GB -p NEW_POOL
[root@localhost rdc]# ssm create -n disk003 --fs xfs -s 3GB -p NEW_POOL
```

Now, let's check our new volumes.

```
[root@localhost rdc]# ssm list
--------------------------------------------------------------------
Device           Free      Used      Total  Pool      Mount point
--------------------------------------------------------------------
/dev/sda                             20.00 GB           PARTITIONED
/dev/sda1                             1.00 GB           /boot
/dev/sda2       0.00 KB  19.00 GB   19.00 GB  cl
/dev/sdb                              6.00 GB
/dev/sdb1       0.00 KB   6.00 GB    6.00 GB  NEW_POOL
/dev/sdc                              4.00 GB
/dev/sdc1    1016.00 MB   3.00 GB    4.00 GB  NEW_POOL
--------------------------------------------------------------------

--------------------------------------------------------------------
Pool       Type   Devices       Free       Used      Total
--------------------------------------------------------------------
NEW_POOL   lvm    2        1016.00 MB    9.00 GB    9.99 GB
cl         lvm    1           0.00 KB   19.00 GB   19.00 GB
--------------------------------------------------------------------

--------------------------------------------------------------------------------
Volume                 Pool      Volume size  FS     FS size      Free   Type    Mount point
--------------------------------------------------------------------------------
/dev/cl/root           cl          17.00 GB   xfs   16.99 GB   13.04 GB  linear  /
/dev/cl/swap           cl           2.00 GB
/dev/NEW_POOL/disk001  NEW_POOL     3.00 GB   xfs    2.99 GB    2.99 GB  linear
/dev/NEW_POOL/disk003  NEW_POOL     3.00 GB   xfs    2.99 GB    2.99 GB  linear
/dev/NEW_POOL/disk002  NEW_POOL     3.00 GB   xfs    2.99 GB    2.99 GB  linear
/dev/sda1                           1.00 GB   xfs  1014.00 MB  786.99 MB  part    /boot
--------------------------------------------------------------------------------
[root@localhost rdc]# 
```

We now have three separate logical volumes spanned across two physical disk partitions.

Logical volumes are a powerful feature now built into CentOS Linux. We have touched the surface on managing these. Mastering pools and logical volumes come with practice and extended learning. For now, you have learned the basics of LVM management in CentOS and possess the ability to create basic striped Logical Volumes on a single host.

www.ingramcontent.com/pod-product-compliance
Lightning Source LLC
LaVergne TN
LVHW051245050326
832903LV00028B/2583